God and Man
at Georgetown Prep

D1637430

God and Man
at Georgetown Prep

HOW I BECAME A CATHOLIC DESPITE
20 YEARS OF CATHOLIC SCHOOLING

MARK GAUVREAU JUDGE

A *Crossroad* Book
The Crossroad Publishing Company
New York

The Crossroad Publishing Company
16 Penn Plaza, Suite 1550, New York, NY 10001

Copyright © 2005 by Mark Gauvreau Judge

All rights reserved. No part of this book may be reproduced, stored in a retrieval system, or transmitted, in any form or by any means, electronic, mechanical, photocopying, recording, or otherwise, without the written permission of The Crossroad Publishing Company.

Printed in the United States of America

This text of this book is set in 10.5/13 Goudy Old Style.
The display face is Nuptial.

Library of Congress Cataloging-in-Publication Data
Judge, Mark Gauvreau, 1964–
    God and man at Georgetown Prep : how I became a Catholic despite 20 years of Catholic schooling / Mark Gauvreau Judge.
       p. cm.
    Includes bibliographical references and index.
    ISBN 0-8245-2313-X (alk. paper)
    1. Judge, Mark Gauvreau, 1964– 2. Catholics – United States – Biography.
I. Title.
BX4705.J765A3 2005
282′.092 – dc22

                                      2005006981

1 2 3 4 5 6 7 8 9 10   10 09 08 07 06 05

For My Father and
Rev. Gregory Hartley, SJ
Mentors in Christ

Contents

— Chapter One —

My Dad the Catholic

My father had been dead for several months before it dawned on me that he'd been a Catholic.

It should have been easy to figure out that Dad was Catholic. He went to Catholic Mass every Sunday. He owned a St. Joseph's daily missal book, the same one he had had since he was a kid. He could read Latin, and even though he wrote for a scientific magazine, *National Geographic*, his journalism was garnished with Christian references. He had gone to three Catholic schools in Washington, where he lived: Blessed Sacrament, the Jesuit all-boys school Gonzaga, and the Catholic University of America. His favorite book was one with heavy Catholic overtones, *The Lord of the Rings*.

And yet, in the summer of 1996, I found myself surprised to finally realize that my dad had been deeply, seriously, and mystically Catholic. He believed in the supernatural world and believed that we could catch glimpses of it in this world. He saw in nature not only beauty but the face of Christ.

In all my years of Catholic schooling I had never heard or read anything that brought these worlds together — that explained Catholicism as a religion about both faith and reason, about the reality of this world and of the next. I always considered my father's mysticism, his love of nature and poetry and beauty, to be the sign of a brilliant man who occasionally had his head in the clouds. No one ever explained that his mysticism may have been the sign of someone whose feet were planted firmly in reality.

Then I started going through Dad's old stuff in the basement, and I came across some books: G. K. Chesterton's *Orthodoxy*, Thomas Merton's *The Seven Storey Mountain* and *No Man Is an Island*, prayer

1

and meditation books from the 1940s, a biography of Cardinal Newman.

I picked up Chesterton's *Orthodoxy* and for the first time began to understand Dad's Catholicism. I was stunned by one passage in particular:

> Mysticism keeps men sane. As long as you have mystery you have health; when you destroy mystery you create morbidity. The ordinary man has always been sane because the ordinary man has always been a mystic. He has permitted the twilight. He has always had one foot in earth and the other in fairyland. . . . He has always cared more for truth than for consistency. If he saw two truths that seemed to contradict each other, he would take the two truths and the contradiction along with them. His spiritual sight is stereoscopic, like his physical sight: he sees two pictures at once and yet sees all the better for that. Thus he has always believed there was such a thing as fate, but such a thing as free will also. . . . The morbid logician seeks to make everything lucid, and succeeds in making everything mysterious. The mystic allows one thing to be mysterious, and everything else becomes lucid. . . . As we have taken the circle as the symbol of reason and madness, we may take the cross as a symbol at once of mystery and of health. Buddhism is centripetal, but Christianity is centrifugal: it breaks out. . . . The circle returns upon itself and is bound. The cross opens its arms to the four winds; it is a signpost for free travelers.

I was thunderstruck — not only by the brilliance of the prose, which in a flash made me understand more about Christianity than almost twenty years of Catholic schooling had, but by the realization that this passage beautifully summed up my father. In my mind Dad was many things: an intellectual and scholar, an explorer, a hilarious — and occasionally bawdy — Irish storyteller who could keep a room rapt with attention for an hour, and someone who loved rock and roll. In my mind, none of those things were Catholic. Being Catholic was going to Mass and to confession. It was old priests and strict nuns. It had nothing to do with philosophy, science, love, or anything else worthwhile in the world. It was the religion I had left behind in high school.

Yet here, in Chesterton's great masterpiece about Christianity, was the spirit, and the brilliance, of my father. As I pored through his things, I began to reflect on his life, trying to pinpoint exactly where, besides Chesterton, his Catholicism had come from. The son of a professional baseball player for the Washington Senators, Dad had been a "whiz kid" on the radio in the 1930s and at a young age had fallen in love with literature, devouring everything from classics such as the *Iliad* to what were then-new books such as *The Lord of the Rings* and *The Chronicles of Narnia*. He had a book of poems published when he was sixteen. Dad went to Catholic University in Washington, where he was editor of the *Tower*, the school newspaper. There he met a fellow student, Fred Maroon, a photographer. The two men became colleagues and close friends, working together in 1950 as coeditors of the *Cardinal*, the school yearbook. The book won a national competition, and my dad and Maroon were hired by *Life* magazine, whose staff referred to Judge and Maroon as "the gold dust twins" because of their flair for financially successful ventures. The two men loved Washington, however, and soon moved back from New York. "I remember the first time I saw Joe's bedroom," Maroon wrote in the CUA magazine after my father died. "Every one of his four walls was lined with books, which prompted me to ask cynically how many he had actually read. 'All of them,' he answered. And knowing Joe, I believe he remembered everything in them. He was a walking encyclopedia, and his curiosity and interests were universal."

After a few years in Washington working for a local television station and then the Department of Labor, my father landed a job with *National Geographic* in 1962, two years before I was born. He would be there for the rest of his life. He wrote about places all over the world — Boston, Jerusalem, Ireland, Disney World. In the 1980s, after years of research, he discovered the landing site where Columbus touched down in the New World. His press conference in 1986 announcing the discovery garnered the most coverage of any in the storied history of the magazine. In his work at the magazine — he rose to associate editor — he could on one day talk to his friend Stephen

Jay Gould about evolution, then a day later take me to Emmitsburg, Maryland, to visit a woman who claimed to be in communication with the Virgin Mary.

Dad loved nature, which, as I imagined, was not a really Catholic philosophy. He could name every flower in the garden and every constellation in the night sky above our house in Potomac, Maryland. He knew every type of bird and would spend mornings on the C&O Canal that runs by the Potomac River, softly padding along the path and bird-watching through his binoculars. As kids we would make fun of him, imitating his incredible knowledge. "That's a mockingbird," I would say, pointing to a random bird in the front yard of our suburban house. I had no idea what kind of bird it was, but I knew I would soon find out. "That's no mockingbird," Dad would say. "That's a junco."

Being Catholic was going to Mass and to confession. It was old priests and strict nuns.

Another clue to Dad's faith came when I found his old high school yearbook from Gonzaga, the Jesuit boys' school in Washington he had attended. The 1944 edition of the *Aetonian* offers this foreword from the students:

> With Christ as our ideal, we the class of forty-four are about to plunge into a world of chaos and war. We now begin the task of accomplishing our mission as educated Christian citizens; no longer the hesitating boys of our freshman days, but approved products of a Catholic, Christian education.
>
> The proper and intimate meaning of the words "Christian Education" is too often lost in technicalities. The big thing to remember is that a Christian education strives primarily at fashioning a man after the fascinating stature of Christ. An education so founded on Christ, far from diminishing human life and its beauty, rather enriches it and elevates by drawing it gradually to the ideal of Christian and human perfection.

Its finished product should be a second Christ in his spiritual and temporal strivings, a devout, intelligent and practical man. To form, then, a man of harmoniously developed Christlike personality was the ultimate aim of our education. In Christ Jesus, and in Him alone, we discover all the qualities of the ideal personality. Being God, He is all-just, all-holy, all-knowing, and particularly, all-merciful; being man he is the delightful human expression of all these qualities.

In a couple of paragraphs, the teenage authors of the 1944 *Aetonian* had done what most teachers in my twenty years of Catholic education had not: wedded Catholicism and humanism. The authors pinpoint a central truth of Catholicism, one that would be emphasized by the future pope John Paul II: the way to be truly and fully human is to emulate Christ. In a few words the secular rift, all too common among modern Catholics, was exposed. To many of us, Catholicism had been a compartment in our lives, the Sunday Mass obligation and the imperative to be nice to people. Our strivings at work, in romance, and with our families were the real world, and the church could say nothing to our desires for material goods, love, and security — the things that really made us human.

As I went through more of Dad's old books, again and again I found myself surprised at how, for so many old Catholic writers, there was no divide between the church and the world. Dad's embrace of nature was explained in a passage from *No Man Is an Island,* the 1955 book of meditations by the Trappist monk Thomas Merton:

All nature is meant to make us think of paradise. Woods, fields, valleys, hills, the rivers and the sea, the clouds traveling across the sky, light and darkness, sun and stars, remind us that the world was first created as a paradise for the first Adam, and that in spite of his sin and ours, it will once again become a paradise when we are all risen from death in the second Adam. Heaven is even now mirrored in created things.

Reading these books, I began to understand a crucial difference between my father's faith and the faith of modern Catholics. It was described well by Frank Sheed, a great twentieth-century Catholic writer. In his classic *Theology and Sanity,* Sheed noted that many older Catholics consider their faith to be as close and personal as the clothes they are wearing. To them, the world is represented by a few patches on their clothes.

To many modern Catholics, the world is the clothes they wear, their Catholicism the patches. To us, the supernatural is not the prism through which we view the world; the world is the prism through which we view the supernatural. We consider this latter position the more realistic and intellectual one. Yet in my father's books I found men and women who felt that the way to get to the real was through God. This was eloquently explained in another of Dad's old books, *The Intellectual Life: Its Spirits, Conditions, Methods.* It was written in 1920 by the French monk A. G. Sertillanges and has this passage describing the meaning of being an intellectual:

> The intellectual I have in view is a man of wide and varied knowledge complementary to a special study thoroughly pursued; he loves the arts and natural beauty; his mind shows itself to be one in everyday occupations and in meditation; he is the same man in the presence of God, of his fellows, and of his maid, carrying within him a world of ideas and feelings that are not only written down in books and in discourses, but flow into his conversation with his friends, and guide his life.
>
> At bottom, everything is connected and everything is the same thing. Intellectuality admits no compartments. All the objects of our thought are so many doors into the "secret garden," the "wine cellar" which is the goal of ardent research. Thoughts and activities, realities and their reflections, all have one and the same Father. Philosophy, art, travel, domestic cares, finance, poetry, and tennis can be allied with one another, and conflict only through lack of harmony.
>
> What is necessary every moment is to be where we ought to be and to do the thing that matters. Everything makes one harmony in the concert of the human and the divine.

I finally began to understand how my dad loved everything from the stars to the oceans, books, women, and flowers — even the Washington Redskins football team and rock and roll. Dad was the biggest Redskins fan I ever knew. He had grown up with the team, watching them play at old Griffith Stadium (where his father played first base for the Senators in the summer), and would never concede that the team was having a lousy season. He would sit in his study and calculate the exact circumstances under which the "Skins" could achieve a playoff berth. He would enter the family room, where we were waiting for the TV broadcast to begin, and announce, "They can do it. If the Cowboys lose to the Raiders by more than fifty-seven points, and we beat Dallas by more than thirty, we're in." He wasn't joking. When we would shout him down as delusional, he always played his trump card. "Seventy-three to nothing," he would remind us, silencing the room. That was the amount by which the Redskins had once lost to the Chicago Bears in 1940 — and proof to Dad that any score was conceivable. It was the greatest loss in Washington football history, a disgrace so profound that it made its way into the Bears fight song. (The song refers to the famous Chicago "T formation," which had never been used before the Washington game and completely baffled the Redskins.) One of the few times I ever heard my mother genuinely angry with Dad was when the Redskins made it to the Super Bowl in 1983. The night before the game we had a party, and no one made it to bed until 3 a.m. About three hours later, Dad woke the house by blasting on the stereo Washington's football fight song, "Hail to the Redskins." Mom was not amused.

Dad also loved rock and roll, although never as much as his beloved Big Band music, which he would blast at all hours when he and Mom had dinner parties. He didn't love rock and roll in the superficial way that some parents did, believing that their vague ideas about the music being all about "freedom" and "the beat" gave them currency with their kids. My father had an ear for music. He hated the Rolling Stones — he would leave the room whenever he heard Mick Jagger's voice — but loved jazz and the Beatles. He could not name a single member of any band, but he would often hear a song coming from one of our rooms and ask us what it was. When I told him the Who, the Cars, the Pet Shop Boys, he would say, "That's a good tune." In college I made him tapes of current songs I liked, which he would listen to over and over again. His favorites were love songs. We would sit in his study while he smoked cigars and drank Irish whiskey and I played him the latest tracks. He would become almost ecstatic over the songs that moved him. I'll never forget the night he became almost speechless — a real feat for him — after hearing the anti-drug song "Bad" by the Christian group U2. Dad understood what the rock intelligentsia didn't: that all good things, including good songs, are from Christ. The best songs capture the essence of Christian love. The popular love song is most often about a love so powerful it can conquer time, distance, and death — a love, like the love of Christ, that has dominion over the natural world.

When my dad died he was working on a book about a man who exemplified my father's Catholicism, which was tough, adventurous, and steeped in the belief of the reality of the spirit world. The life of this man, Demetrius Augustine Gallitzin, is also an exotic, bizarre story that Dad thought would make a good movie.

Gallitzin, born in 1770, was the scion of Prince Demetrius Gallitzin, the Russian ambassador to France and later to Holland. Gallitzin *père* was friends with Diderot, Voltaire, and other Enlightenment thinkers. His wife was the Countess Amalie von Schmettau, a devout Catholic and considered by some to be the most brilliant woman in Europe. When her son was seventeen he became Catholic, taking a new name, Augustine.

When he was twenty-two, Gallitzin traveled to the New World. He landed in Baltimore, a center for Catholic life in America, and entered St. Mary's Seminary. He was moved by the needs of the early church in America, which had only a handful of priests to cover the million square miles of the New World. Contrary to the wishes of his friends and relatives back home, Gallitzin decided to devote his life and fortune to his faith. He became a priest in 1795, adopting the alias of Smith so that no one would suspect he was royalty. Gallitzin was sent to Conewago, a tiny outpost in the wilds of what would become western Maryland, western Pennsylvania, and the Shenandoah Valley of Virginia.

While Gallitzin was making his way in the New World, something strange was happening nearby, in a part of what was then Virginia but what is today West Virginia. In the 1790s Adam Livingston, a Lutheran who lived on an estate in the Shenandoah Valley with his wife and children, began to witness strange happenings in and around his house. Cattle died without explanation — a phenomenon that had driven Livingston to move to Virginia from Pennsylvania in the first place. Worse, the house was haunted. The Livingstons were kept awake at night by the sound of galloping horses and wagons charging through their living room. Furniture moved by itself and crockery smashed to the floor.

Most bizarre — and perhaps comedic — was the clipping. The family often heard the sound of shears and scissors, and almost all of the clothing they owned was cut to pieces by the invisible force. Soon the town, many of whose members saw the frightening occurrences themselves, had names for the Livingston estate, including "The Wizard's Clip" and "Cliptown," names still in use today. With the help of a local priest, Gallitzin successfully exorcised the house, and the clipping ended.

Dad, like most of the Catholics of his generation, was a believer in the reality of evil, both in humans and in the spirit world — and a believer that those worlds could and did overlap. To him the supernatural was real, and not something to be trifled with.

Dad never finished his book on the Wizard's Clip, dying when it was only partially done. I didn't know it at the time, but I would come across Gallitzin again — during my return to the Catholic Church years later.

My father accepted the diagnosis of his illness with the same dignity, soul, and humor with which he faced all of his life. He went through chemotherapy and various trips to the doctor without complaint. I sensed that he knew in his heart that his time on earth was coming to an end.

Right up to the time he grew too sick to leave the house, Dad went to daily Mass. I once considered this the typical action of someone who is beginning to panic as the end draws near, a fearful response to the rising of the shroud. Yet now I realize that in those moments he was becoming more fully who he was, a man who trusted completely in Christ. His faith did not change after his diagnosis became worse and his time shorter. That is to say, his trust in Christ did not become desperate, demanding, or hysterical, as often happens to people who are facing death. He didn't offer sanguine scenarios about going home to heaven or knowing that Jesus was waiting for him on the other side with a big bear hug. Of course he hoped for these things, but in the manner of a true old-school Catholic he knew he was about to enter into a mystery. He hoped for heaven and union with Christ but believed that language — even the language he had used so beautifully in his writing — was helpless to explain it. He knew he had reached a place where human things would fall away. He died in the afternoon on April 18, 1996.

Reading my dad's old books, looking through his unfinished manuscript, watching him bird-watching on old videotapes, I began to realize why it was a surprise to me that Dad was Catholic: I am a member of the generation of Catholics raised after Vatican II who were cheated out of a Catholic education. I had made it through twenty years of Catholic schooling without a catechism and without being introduced to Chesterton, Newman, or Maritain, to say nothing of church fathers such as Irenaeus and St. Gregory the Great. Indeed, I had spent most of my life in three of the most prestigious Catholic schools in America — Our Lady of Mercy (a grade school in Potomac, Maryland), Georgetown Prep (the famous Jesuit high school), and the Catholic University of America. In my time at these institutions I was taught virtually nothing about Catholicism. At Our Lady of Mercy in the late 1970s it was my father, not my teachers, who took me to see the new pope, John Paul II. At Georgetown Prep in Maryland — one of the best schools in the country, according to its reputation — I learned nothing of Chesterton, Hillaire Belloc, Augustine or Aquinas. I was, however, bombarded with drugs, alcohol, widespread homosexuality among the clergy, and ever-escalating requests for donations to help the wealthy school build another building. I was never assigned a word by or about Ignatius Loyola, the founder of the Jesuits. At Prep I didn't know who Christopher Dawson, Thomas Merton, or Hans Urs von Balthasar were, but *The Road*

Less Traveled, that dreadful piece of New Age Viagra by M. Scott Peck, was required reading in the graphic sex education class, a class taught by a man who is now an ultra-left-wing radio show host in San Francisco. At Catholic University, many things were never taught, but I was told over and over that the Bible cannot be read literally.

I am a member of the generation of Catholics raised after Vatican II who were cheated out of a Catholic education.

It was only by a fortunate accident (the purchase of a religious magazine for my father in 1995) and a reality that was anything but fortunate (the death of my father) that I would begin to return to the church. Sadly, without these events I may never have discovered the magnificence of Catholicism — its fierce intellectualism, its deep love of the wonder and mystery of the world, its loving invitation to humanity to take a step not into fantasy and fairy tales but into the heart of reality. That reality was denied my generation in the 1970s and 1980s, the richness of Catholicism kept from us by people inside the church itself. They were teachers who for political reasons — not to mention the excitements of modern culture and psychotherapy — refused to teach the best that the faith has to offer. Catholics in my generation suffer from deep religious illiteracy, the result not only of conscious efforts by certain radicals, particularly in the 1960s and 1970s, but by what historian James Hitchcock calls "drift" — the tendency to let traditions dry up through neglect, conscious and not.

What was so tragic is that liberal reformers in the 1960s who almost destroyed Catholic education initially had a good idea. They saw that Catholic education had in many ways become rote and anti-intellectual. To be sure, Catholics in pre–Vatican II days taught the catechism and lived the faith with a brio totally foreign to Catholics today. But they also tended to be so conservative that they often ignored the modern Catholic giants in their midst, rejecting and banning some, like Jacques Maritain, out of irrational fears about modernism, while ignoring a genius like Chesterton out of sheer intellectual laziness. Since at least 1906, popes had warned against all forms of modernism, and the so-called Catholic ghetto in America could be suspicious of anything new, no matter how orthodox it was. The great Catholic thinkers seemed to be appreciated by everyone but Catholics.

Then something significant happened in the 1960s. Liberals called for reform in the name of both the vibrant Christianity of the early church, with its deep humanism and concern for the poor, and the richness of the modern thinkers who had converted to the faith — men like Chesterton and Maritain. Yet these same liberals shifted in midstream, abandoning both and embracing a thoughtless radicalism, leaving us the vanilla Catholicism that I was taught, the same one that today (with a few notable exceptions) continues to stagger through history. Even though I was being raised by a great Catholic intellectual, for most of my life I thought Catholicism was anti-intellectual and had nothing to say about life. Today I realize that genuine Catholicism offers truths deeper and more exciting than our most wonderful dreams, and a philosophical humanism that truly recognizes the staggering reality of God's desire for our love, a love that can exist only in freedom and wedded to the truth. I only wish that, because of the assault on traditional Catholic education in the 1960s and 1970s, Catholic faith hadn't been so difficult to find.

— Chapter Two —

The Collapse

The education of Catholic children prior to the 1960s was far from perfect, but it could not be said the kids didn't know their faith.

From the mid-1930s to 1950, my father went to Washington's best Catholic schools: Blessed Sacrament, Gonzaga, and Catholic University. Dad saved some of his report cards and notebooks from those years, and they reveal a distinctly Catholic curriculum. At Blessed Sacrament, my father's generation memorized the famous *Baltimore Catechism* (famous, at least, in old-school Catholic circles). The *Baltimore Catechism* was authorized in 1884 in the Third Plenary Council of Baltimore and drew heavily on the 1777 Irish Catechism, which itself had been inspired by the Council of Trent. "The basic *Baltimore Catechism* helped form several generations of Catholics in this country during a period when the Catholic faith was most vital and vibrant in the lives of those who professed and tried to live it," observed Msgr. Michael J. Wrenn in his book *Catechisms and Controversies*.

At Gonzaga, Dad and his classmates were required to study Latin, Greek, religion, and Western history (although in those benighted times it was known just as history). They studied Thomas Aquinas, the intellectual father of the church, as well as Ignatius Loyola, the founder of the Jesuits. They read the *Iliad* and the *Odyssey*. Attendance at Mass was mandatory, and prayer was said before every class. There were three hours of homework every night. By the time he was a senior, Dad could read Latin fluently. At Catholic University he became the editor of the newspaper; he sprinkled his editorials with classical references that he could take for granted the student body would understand. He understood the two cities of Western culture, Athens and Jerusalem. Forty years later, at Georgetown Prep, the prestigious Maryland Jesuit school, I learned about the female body, heard from New Age writers that I could create my own theological system, and learned about life in English class by reading *The Catcher in the Rye*.

I also — however politically incorrect it is to say so — didn't have teachers with the kind of raw masculinity that was common to the priesthood before the 1960s. My favorite historical figure from Dad's schooling is Cornelius Aloysius Herlihy, the prefect of discipline at Gonzaga in the 1940s. Herlihy, nicknamed "Nails" because of his bulldog toughness, was more feared than Stalin. He had broken every knuckle playing football on a glass-strewn lot near the Washington slum where he grew up. He could silence a room full of a hundred rowdy teenage boys simply by appearing in the doorway. He kept a starter gun in his desk, and once fired it at a tardy student, who, poor fellow, didn't know it shot blanks. He would literally pick kids up off the ground by their collar when they were running down stairs, and could drop-kick a football over the five-story school building.

In the yearbook Nails was called "a stirring example of Catholic manhood in action," and there were priests like him all over America. They led the church and its educational system and did not shy away from a fight. In a 1942 speech given to the National Catholic Education Association, the Reverend John A. O'Brien, who at the time was on the faculty of the University of Notre Dame, gave a talk that is unimaginable today. The good reverend was well ahead of his time. The specter of totalitarianism in Nazi Germany and Soviet Russia was only the first threat to civilization, he announced. The second was paganism: Christians "live in a social climate hostile to the Faith," he said, and in a world where such pagan practices as divorce, birth control by contraceptive devices, abortion, euthanasia, and sterilization are hailed as symptoms of modern progress. Not much has changed in sixty years.

O'Brien also gives examples to back up his thesis, and it makes for stunning reading for those of us who might have believed that the culture wars began only in the 1960s. O'Brien carefully goes through stories from magazines, which in those pre-television times were the mass media. A piece in *Reader's Digest* by atheist philosopher

Bertrand Russell offers a way to live without God. *Redbook* runs a piece, "Have You a Religion?," in which evil and the devil are both denied. A piece in *Ladies' Home Journal* pushs "artificial semination." *Cosmopolitan* approves of euthanasia. On November 17, 1941, *Time* pulled a fast one, saying that Pope Leo XII (described as "indignant") had denounced Thomas Jefferson's founding principles of America. In fact, Leo was condemning a secular interpretation of America's founding — a founding that had at least one foot firmly planted on Christian soil. In reply, *Time* acknowledged that O'Brien had made some good points, but declined to print a formal retraction. How little has changed.

By far the most disturbing citation by Father O'Brien came from the *Ladies' Home Journal*. The magazine ran a serial, "Marriage Is a Private Affair," that included quotations from a doctor who advised an ill woman to have an abortion. O'Brien's condemnation is tragic and breathtaking: "One shudders to contemplate the untold thousands of unborn babies who may have been murdered because of this one story." Thousands. It's inconceivable what the good father would think about the tens of millions of babies dead in the intervening decades. O'Brien ends with a summons to action:

> To be forewarned is to be forearmed. Against the rulers of the world of darkness and against the spirits of wickedness in high places we must arm our pupils in schools, as Saint Paul sought to arm the Ephesians, when he said to them: "Therefore take unto you the armor of God, that you may be able to resist in the evil day, and to stand in all things perfect. Stand, therefore, having your loins girt about with truth, and having on the breastplate of justice, and your feet shod with the preparation of the gospel of peace; in all things take the shield of faith, wherewith you may be able to extinguish all the fiery darts of the most wicked one."

For generations of Catholics prior to Vatican II, faith was based on the instruction received from the *Baltimore Catechism*. Using its question-and-answer format, children memorized the answers to hundreds of questions about the meaning of life. In his book *Right from the Beginning,* Pat Buchanan recalls the emphasis that was put on learning the catechism at Blessed Sacrament, the grade school Buchanan attended in the 1940s. Buchanan was chosen to represent his school on a local Catholic radio program and always remembered learning the catechism forward and backward.

"What does the Eighth Commandment forbid?" he was asked.

"The Eighth Commandment forbids lies, rash judgment, detraction, calumny, and telling of secrets we are bound to keep."

"When does a person commit the sin of detraction?"

"A person commits the sin of detraction when, without a good reason, he makes known the hidden faults of another."

Buchanan also makes an additional crucial point: the catechism was just one part of a rich religious life. As Msgr. Michael J. Wrenn observed, "Although these catechisms were all heavily oriented toward imparting the intellectual content of the faith, they were generally used — and it was assumed that they would generally be used — in conjunction with regular and active participation in the sacramental and liturgical life of the church on the part of those being catechized. So it is not true that these catechisms were nothing more than arid, abstract, lifeless summaries of doctrinal formulas with no reference or relevance to the life of the person being catechized." Buchanan's memoir testifies to this rich life of the church. He notes that "virtually every day of the calendar year was a feast day of some particular saint."

One of the most touching moments in Buchanan's memoir took place when his father woke Pat up in the middle of the night to keep him company as he took his turn as a member of the Nocturnal Adoration Society. The society was formed to keep an all-night vigil before the Holy Eucharist and to pray for sinners. The men would pray in shifts, taking turns driving to the church. Buchanan never forgot the night he attended with his father: "Remembering him kneeling there, broad shoulders squared, bald head bent in prayer, in that darkened church, where the only light came from the distant tabernacle beyond the altar rail, I am reminded what the centurion had said to Christ: 'for I too am a man under authority.' "

Like all good Catholics at the time, Buchanan was against totalitarianism — including Communist totalitarianism. It could even
be claimed that the church was the first true anticommunist force
in America. A prime mover was Edmund Walsh, a Jesuit priest at
Georgetown University. Walsh was born in Boston in 1885, the son
of a policeman and second-generation American. He earned a scholarship to Boston College High School, and after graduating in 1902
he entered the Jesuit novitiate in Frederick, Maryland. From 1909 to
1912 Walsh taught in the high school section of Georgetown University. On May 12, 1912, he heard a speech at the university that
profoundly affected him. It was delivered during a dedication ceremony for the unveiling of a statue of John Carroll, America's first
bishop and the founder of Georgetown. At the ceremony, speaker
Edward D. White, a Supreme Court chief justice, made a connection
between John Carroll and Carroll's brother Charles, a signer of the
Declaration of Independence. White held that Georgetown University and the United States of America were founded on the same
Christian principles: natural law, the rights of man, reason, faith.
Walsh never forgot the speech.

Walsh was ordained a priest in 1916. In 1919, after World War I,
he founded the Georgetown School of Foreign Service. In February
1922, Walsh went to Rome, where he was assigned to the Papal Relief
Mission to Russia. Russia, having undergone a revolution five years
earlier, was in the midst of a famine that would claim over five million
victims by the end of 1922. Russia was also in the midst of a purge of
Catholic clergy, and the Holy See gave Walsh authority to negotiate
on behalf of clerical prisoners.

What Walsh saw in the new Soviet Union stunned him. The new
government was using the famine as an excuse to loot churches and
arrest clergy. In 1922 twenty-eight bishops and over twelve hundred
priests were murdered or executed. In his diary of May 1922, Walsh
saw the future. Russia wasn't in trouble, he wrote — the world was.
He expressed "fear for the consequences in the economic, the political, the social, the religious, and educational orders of the entire
world." Communism was "the most reactionary and savage school of
thought known to history," bringing with it a "reign of terror that

makes the French Revolution insignificant." After all, he reasoned, the French Revolution was limited to France. The Bolsheviks, however, envisioned "World Revolution, or in other words, universal Socialism with its concomitants — no state, no government, no belief in God, no marriages, no religion or, in a word, the total destruction of the present Christian civilization and the substitution of the Communist state."

By 1923, the relief mission was feeding 158,000 Russians a day. But this didn't stop the religious purges. For most of the early 1920s, the Russian Orthodox Church had been the target, but in 1923 the Bolsheviks turned their attention to the Catholic Church. On March 3, 1923, troops in Petrograd arrested the Catholic archbishop and fourteen priests. They were sent to Moscow to stand trial before the Supreme Revolutionary Tribunal. Walsh complained bitterly about the show trials. Two of the clergy, including the Polish vicar-general, Monsignor Constantine Budkiewicz, were sentenced to death and the others to extended prison sentences.

On April 5, 1923, Walsh wrote to a friend back home:

> The week of the Passion is truly a week of the Passion in the capital city of the Bolsheviks. As the whole Christian world knows, this week signaled the beginning of a veritable Neronian persecution, prepared long before and now being actually carried out... that the communists and atheists might show their triumphant power, for they have constantly sought the destruction of all religion among the Russians.

There were those who rejected Walsh's eyewitness accounts of the new Russia. In May 1923, the *Nation* published an article by the Reverend John Haynes Holmes. Holmes outright denied the persecution in Russia, claiming that he had just been to Russia and "looked in vain for evidence of such atrocities." In a *New York Times* interview, Percy Stickney Grant, a Methodist pastor, claimed that the clergy in Russia were not persecuted.

Walsh and later the Catholic Church in general (it took the church into the 1930s to begin attacking Communism with full force) were appalled by this moral obtuseness. Fulton Sheen, a priest and radio personality, wrote entire books and gave sermons on the evils of Bolshevism. Cardinal Francis Spellman, archbishop of New York, warned his city and the rest of the country about the Soviet threat. James M. Gillis, the Paulist editor of *Catholic World* magazine, condemned "the liberal press, which pretends to admire martyrdom and to adore fidelity to principle, but couldn't recognize spiritual heroism when face to face with it. It has no rebukes for the persecutors, and no word for the martyrs except insinuation, innuendo, and false accusation."

> *Catholic liberals would also express hostility to thought itself, but their attack would be on the accumulated wisdom of thousands of years of church teaching.*

All this changed. By the 1960s and 1970s Catholic anti-communism had become Catholic anti-anti-communism. In 1971 the *National Catholic Reporter* published an article, "Distrust of Church in Cuba Fades," that claimed that Catholics had come to embrace the government of Cuba, which allowed them to live as real Christians for the first time. In 1974, Cuban exiles in America asked the United States Catholic Conference to denounce human rights violations in Cuba as well as Chile and Brazil; a conference official replied that he knew of no violations. In 1977 ninety Americans who had protested the Vietnam War issued a statement calling on the Communist government in Vietnam to end its oppression. Priests Daniel and Philip Berrigan were angry, claiming that the former South Vietnamese government was worse than the Communists: "There is a great difference between reeducation camps and tiger cages," the brothers said in a statement. Minnesota priest Harry Bury visited Vietnam in 1972 and announced that people there "are free to worship, free to teach religion, free to care for the poor and those in need. They are not completely free to criticize the North Vietnamese government. But neither are we in the United States." In 1977, *Commonweal* published an article about the totalitarian regime in Cambodia. The author told readers to be "cautiously optimistic" about the new regime "or just shut up."

What Walsh, Gillis, and the Catholic Church were facing in Soviet defenders was not so much opinion as what would mar the church beginning in the 1960s and guide my own radical politics in the 1980s: hostility to thought itself. The phrase "hostility to thought itself" comes from the historian Robert Conquest, author of a brilliant book about totalitarianism, *Reflections on a Ravaged Century*. Conquest outlines the thought that gave rise to Nazism and Communism — and the hostility to thought that led far too many Western intellectuals and artists to defend Soviet crimes. Conquest broke down the arguments defending Communism into four basic steps:

1. There is much injustice under capitalism.

2. Socialism will end this injustice.

3. Therefore anything that supports socialism is to be supported,

4. Including any amount of injustice.

Some of the things said by Western intellectuals in defense of Stalinism were truly appalling. In the 1920s, writer Lincoln Steffens traveled to Russia, returned home, and declared, "I have seen the future and it works." Playwright George Bernard Shaw went to Russia during the height of the famine in the early 1930s; he then returned home and described the Soviet population as overfed. In 1934, H. G. Wells had a private audience with Stalin. Wells declared that he, Wells, had "never met a man more candid, fair, and honest," adding that "no one is afraid of him and everyone trusts him." Conquest notes that many American "suckers...did not take in what they saw with their own eyes." Writer Malcolm Muggeridge also saw this phenomenon, describing "Quakers applauding task parades, feminists delighted at the sight of women bowed under a hundredweight of coal, architects in ecstasies over ramshackle buildings just erected and already crumbling away." Most notoriously, *New York Times* reporter Walter Duranty didn't just play down the famine that killed ten million in the Ukraine. He denied it outright, claiming that such claims were "malignant propaganda." Duranty won the Pulitzer Prize.

This was not a group of people doing something wonderful, expressing their opinions and adding their wisdom to the marketplace of ideas. This is what Conquest calls it: a "morbid affliction" or even an "addiction" to an ideology that was so obviously criminal. Yet, as Conquest notes, simply calling these people unpatriotic does not get to the heart of the problem. In fact, it can be a diversion. Calling someone unpatriotic allows that person access to the grab bag of countercharges: the accuser is accused of being McCarthyist, hostile to dissent, against the great American tradition of protest, attempting censorship, and so forth. It's like saying that someone is a bad Catholic. The accused immediately dons the mantle of victim, and it often works. Conquest points to the real problem:

> Many whose allegiance went to the Soviet Union may well be seen as traitors to their countries, and to the democratic culture. But their profounder fault was more basic still. Seeing themselves as independent brains, making their choices as thinking beings, they ignored their own criteria. They did not examine the multifarious evidence, already available in the 1930s, on the realities of the Communist regimes. That is to say, they were traitors to the human mind, to thought itself.

This hostility to thought itself was difficult to shake long after the 1930s, as Father Walsh witnessed. Until he had a stroke in 1952, Walsh's primary goal was to convince anyone who would listen that Communism was an evil, expansionist, totalitarian system that was the most serious danger to the Western world and Christianity. He died in 1956, by which point Catholic anticommunism was starting to crack. The crack became a canyon during the Vietnam War, when many Catholics were not so much ambivalent as hostile to America and sympathetic to Communists. America was not in a losing but honorable battle against a totalitarian regime — indeed, an heir of Stalin — but was the evil force in the war. Student protestors didn't call for America's retreat; they openly praised the Vietcong.

Catholic liberals would also express hostility to thought itself, but their attack would be on the accumulated wisdom of thousands of years of church teaching. But before Catholic liberals turned into ideologues, they mounted a largely honest and intellectually sound critique of the church. In many ways the church in the early part of the twentieth century was indeed insular and narrow-minded. Catholics, many of whom were immigrants or the sons and daughters of immigrants, stuck together as a clan. They were uneducated and deferential to the pope, as well as deeply mistrustful of modernity. In a speech given to the 1942 assembly of the National Catholic Education Association by Brother George N. Schuster from the South Side Catholic School in St. Louis, the good brother offered a biting critique of what was then called Catholic Book Week, which used to be held the first week of November. The school put up posters and invited a Catholic writer to speak, but the students could hardly wait for it to end to get back to "real" literature. At the end of the week, noted Schuster, "we feel relieved with the relief of foreigners who for an entire week have been walking in a strange land, unable to speak its language, unacquainted with the geography, with no enthusiasm for its people or its scenery." He goes on:

> We must first read ourselves into some degree of understanding and appreciation of our Catholic literary heritage. Have we ever considered the divine origin and sublime mission of Catholic letters? Have we ever thought of Catholic literature as springing from the God-Man who in the beginning was the Word that grew strong in wisdom and knowledge before God and man, the mature Word that looked down through the centuries even to you and me and said: "Go, teach all nations"?
>
> Have we ever considered the illustrious army of men and women who were fired by that command to make truth and beauty manifest the world over, those makers of our heritage through the ages: Peter and Paul, Jerome and Augustine, Bede and Benedict, Alfred and Charlemagne, Anselm and Hildebrand, Aquinas and Dante, More and Teresa and Ignatius, Newman and Leo XII and Chesterton?

In fact, when Brother Schuster was speaking the church was in the middle of a great intellectual renaissance. Thinkers such as Chesterton, Hillaire Belloc, Evelyn Waugh, Jacques Maritain, Etienne Gilson — and, in a few years, Thomas Merton — had converted to Catholicism. J. R. R. Tolkien was writing *The Lord of the Rings*.

Gilson and Maritain spearheaded the neo-Thomistic revival, a re-discovery of the teaching of Thomas Aquinas — or rather a discovery of what were thought to be the liberal, intellectual arguments of St. Thomas. (The conservatives thought of Thomas as a rock of tradition.) Thomism had gained something of a stranglehold on Catholic thought, however, blocking out all other philosophies. Perhaps the most depressing case of strict Thomism not recognizing a genius was that of Dietrich von Hildebrand.

Von Hildebrand was the son of the famous German sculptor Adolf von Hildebrand, who created the "Father Rhine" and Wittlesbach fountains in Munich. (Adolf von Hildebrand's father, Bruno, was one of the first people to see the bunk in Marxist economic theory, a distinction that earned him a mention in Paul Johnson's book *Intellectuals*.) In Florence, Adolf von Hildebrand raised his family; his six children were all girls except for the youngest, Dietrich.

Young Dietrich's life was suffused with the finest art and culture in the world, yet something was different about him: unlike his parents and siblings, he was religious. When Dietrich was a boy, one of his sisters took him to a church to view the art, and Dietrich insisted on genuflecting before every altar. When he was fourteen, his sister Eva informed him that moral values are relative. Dietrich argued against her, even challenging his father, who thought his son was just being a petulant fourteen-year-old. Dietrich retorted that an argument based on the age of one's opponent was no argument at all.

While studying at the University of Munich in 1907 von Hildebrand met Max Scheler, the great German Catholic philosopher and father of phenomenology, a school of thought that would also deeply influence the future John Paul II. Von Hildebrand was enchanted by Scheler's passion and charisma, and he converted to the Catholic Church.

When the Nazis came to power, von Hildebrand fled to Vienna, where he published an anti-Nazi newspaper. While there he also wrote *Transformation in Christ*, one of the greatest books ever written. *Transformation in Christ* details the steps to be taken to become a faithful and fully realized Christian. It covers virtually every human behavior and psychology, including germ phobia and shyness. One small insight von Hildebrand offers speaks to the problem of Catholicism over the course of the twentieth century: rote conservatism that is uninformed by Christ, and radicalism that seeks to topple all tradition for no good reason. The conventionalist is Catholic "because his parents and his ancestors also were Catholics; because it is the thing to comply with one's duties toward the Church — not because the Church is the surviving Christ and the depository of infallible doctrinal authority." Like the conventionalist, the Bohemian "takes the divine commandments and the demands implied in true values for mere human statutes.... He is just as ignorant of the true nature of divine commandments and genuine values as is the conventionalist."

Dissenters such as Michael Novak were faithful to the church in a way that would today be described as conservative.

Von Hildebrand barely escaped from Vienna with his life — his wife Alice writes about this compellingly in her book *The Soul of a Lion* — and he secured a teaching position at Fordham. There he ran into a problem. In February 1943 the administration attempted to fire him, claiming that von Hildebrand was a non-Thomist. Von Hildebrand's department boss, Father Hunter Guthrie, SJ, balked at the request. Von Hildebrand kept his job.

For too many American Catholics, this distrust of non-Thomistic intellectualism — and often any form of intellectualism — was a way of life. In his 1988 book *The Reshaping of Catholicism*, Avery Dulles notes that "the American Catholic community in those days was not conspicuous for its intellectual and cultural life. Its cultural features were borrowed for the most part from the Catholic countries of Western Europe." Catholics, observes Dulles, "tended to look upon the Middle Ages as the golden age of faith."

Ironically, many of the liberals who would cause so much trouble for the church in the 1960s and ruin Catholic education began as champions of both early Christianity and the twentieth-century intellectual renaissance — a renaissance that was full of orthodox

Catholics such as Chesterton and von Hildebrand. In his 1964 book
A New Generation: American and Catholic, Michael Novak, who
would become a conservative in the 1980s, links the revival with the
activist popes of the previous hundred years, beginning with Pope
Leo XIII in 1878. Leo himself had called for a rediscovery and renewal of St. Thomas. Novak argues that the Catholic renewal that
followed was perfectly in keeping with the traditions of the church —
in fact, it was actually an attempt to return to the genuine roots of
the church. As Novak writes, "No one accident did so much harm
to the Catholic renewal before the council, as the epithet 'liberal'
affixed to its leaders. Far from flirting with the current of thought
generated by the Enlightenment and the social-intellectual thinking
of the avant-garde nonbeliever, these leaders are the most active in
striving to regain the Catholic tradition." Novak emphasized that it
was the new breed of believers who were doing research into the
earliest theology of the church.

As if to establish his *bona fides* as a Catholic, Novak devotes an
entire chapter of *A New Generation* to a critical look at modern intellectuals. He approvingly cites John Alsop and Louis Bromfield's 1952
definition of the intellectual as an "egghead." Alsop and Bromfield
described the modern intellectual as "faceless, unemotional, but a
little bit haughty and condescending." As well as "a doctrinaire supporter of middle European socialism . . . a bleeding heart," the egghead
is also dominant in American culture: "For years there was almost
no such thing as a conservative intellectual . . . and it is hard to be
a conservative in a country that lives so much in the future as does
America. . . . As a result, when the liberal is not self-critical, there
has been almost no force to check him and make him reevaluate his
positions."

The liberal was also trapped in a paradox; "he was extremely critical of modern American society, with its bland suburbs, bureaucracy,
gray flannel suits, and mechanization, yet was himself promoting
a philosophy that had led to those conditions." It was "his enlightenment that conceived of the new purpose of civilization as
the bringing of maximum contentment to the greatest number by
concrete changes in the environment."

Dissenters such as Michael Novak were faithful to the church in a way that would today be described as conservative. While there were many on the Right who were intolerant of any changes in the church, others seemed to acknowledge and even tire of the climate of anti-intellectualism in the church. It should be said as well that many of the conservatives had good reason to mistrust the direction of liberal American culture, foreseeing in the signs of the times the current return to paganism and the tragedy of abortion.

Liberals in the pre-1960s church hoped for a return to the existential Christianity of the early church and the thought of Thomas Aquinas. They defended the pope — indeed, many Catholic liberals in the 1950s made their case for social change based on papal encyclicals. "It was commonplace for liberals of the 1950s to complain that Rome was far ahead of the American Bishops on most questions," wrote the Catholic historian James Hitchcock in 1971, "and it was often implied that greater loyalty to the Pope would cure the American Church's worst problems."

Just before the Second Vatican Council opened in 1962, *Commonweal* magazine ran a series of articles by American intellectuals and reformers. The proposals are stunning — at least in hindsight — for their modesty. Writers argued for a partially vernacular liturgy and a greater role for the laity in the parishes. Only one writer addressed birth control, but quickly added that he was not questioning the church's judgment; rather he simply found the teaching of the rhythm method presented with too much negativity.

Reformers such as Daniel Callahan and Michael Novak both defended the authority of the church prior to the council. In 1962 *Commonweal,* which would become a liberal magazine after the council, announced that criticism of the church by liberals "must not be bitter; it must be based on love and loyalty to the Church." Callahan even criticized leftist Catholic Garry Wills, finding some of the writing "polemical, cutting, downright unpleasant at times."

At the same time, there were overtures from authorities in the church toward the reformers. In a remarkable sermon "Christ, the Divine Intellectual," given in 1955, Cardinal John J. Wright lamented the lack of intellectuals in the church. Wright claimed that "Catholics have conformed to the prevailing mood of anti-intellectualism in our land," adding that "it would be not only disastrous but also a bitter irony if any school of thought, preoccupied exclusively with the virtues of the will, even sublime virtues so saving as obedience and so noble as loyalty, were to gain such ascendancy among the sons and daughters of the church as to set at naught or almost annihilate the intellectual tradition in the household of the faith." Wright went so far as to advise that "perhaps it is needed that we be slow to label revolutionaries or liberals in any unfavorable sense who have many ideas, including occasional disturbing ideas, instead of a more comfortable few — or none."

Wright may have regretted what we wished for, as the reformers of Vatican II metamorphosed into radicals, and even the catechism of those having only a "comfortable few" ideas was abandoned. The reformers kept moving the goalposts while denying or ignoring that a personal crisis of faith might have been at the heart of their troubles. Michael Novak's journey was typical. In October 1962 Novak re-ported, in the pages of *Commonweal*, his "joy" when the church historian Gabriel Marcel spoke at Harvard. In 1963 Novak called for more Newman clubs on college campuses, claiming that "it is not the believer but the unbeliever who is in danger if a living, in-tellectual faith comes to the campus." By 1965, Novak was starting to change. In his writings he was expressing admiration for secular students. By 1968 Novak was claiming that Christian virtues were open to non-Christians and could best be discovered outside of the Catholic Church.

What happened in the 1960s was not that liberals didn't get all the changes they wanted, but that they shifted positions. Many of the things they wanted were implemented. This left the radicals unsat-isfied, which in turn led to more demands for even further change. They wanted the Mass in English and not Latin, and got it. They wanted less emphasis on tradition and more on helping the poor and social change, and got it. Later they started demanding acceptance of homosexuality and began dabbling in Marxism, forgetting entirely the experience — indeed the person — of Father Walsh.

Daniel Callahan, a Catholic layman and popular author, summed things up in 1967: "The faster the change, the faster [the reformers] raise their sights: Any slowdown, any obstacle, brings on a quick state of funk. At the same time it is turning out that a new liturgy, a new theology, a new biblical exegesis, a new collegiality, don't necessarily produce the kind of rejuvenation everyone thought they would. That unexpected revelation has driven many back to the more basic issues: God, belief, the meaning (if any) of himself." Callahan knew the problem from the inside; like Novak, he had journeyed from orthodoxy to radicalism.

The reason that the Catholic radicals were unhappy, even as the church went through Vatican II, might have had more to do with psychology than theology. James Hitchcock noted as much in his 1971 book *The Decline and Fall of Radical Catholicism.* The radicals, wrote Hitchcock, "are trying to find themselves, and they wish to use the Church for this purpose." The attitude was "directed at personal therapy rather than institutional reform." For this reason the 1960s reformers were increasingly unhappy even as the church became more liberal. Hitchcock put his finger on it: "It is the discovery of the empty spaces within himself, rather than the empty spaces in the Church, which is profoundly demoralizing."

In the process, Catholic education was destroyed as my generation was entering the Catholic schools.

— Chapter Three —

Mercy

In 1964, the year I was born, Mary Perkins Ryan, a prolific journalist for several Catholic periodicals, published the book *Are Parochial Schools the Answer?* Ryan begins with the good news: "A generous laity, crowded churches, and more men regularly attending services than in almost any other country; seminaries and novitiates are filled with candidates." Moreover, "The typical Catholic is no longer poor, ignorant, un-American." This all seems reason for celebration, but Ryan proclaims a dark undercurrent to the wave of success:

> According to this [optimistic] way of thinking, the fact that so many young Catholics seem bored with religion and cynical about the priestly or religious life; or that so many Catholics hold laissez-faire economic ideals condemned by the Church, and right-wing social doctrines completely at odds with papal teaching; or that so many are uninterested in the problems of racial injustice, in society's caring for the sick and aged, in the desperate plight of peoples in other parts of the world; or that there is a continual leakage from the Church, again of unknown proportions — all of this is to be blamed on the influence of modern "secularism."

Rather than wrestling with the modern world, the church fell back on what she had always prescribed: "Providing Mass and the sacraments as conveniently as possible; encouraging devotions old and new, along with spiritual 'refreshers' in the forms of retreats and missions; inveighing against immoral modern practices such as birth control and indecent dress; and fostering the Catholic school system as the very heart of the church's endeavor to keep its children true to the faith in the dangerous maelstrom of modern life."

Ryan represented a clear shift in attitude regarding Catholics and how they viewed the catechism and the modern world. In the beginning of Christianity, of course, the catechism was simply the spreading of the "good news" about Jesus Christ. From the earliest church, authoritative teachings were to be memorized and cherished by the faithful. The good news was often known as *kerygma,* a Greek word for proclamation, and was coupled with the Apostles' Creed, the recital of which was perhaps the earliest form of catechism.

In the early 1960s, a new kerygmatic movement sprang up in the church, and it would be a spark that led to the downfall of the catechism. Spearheaded by priests such as the Australian Jesuits Johannes Hofinger and Josef Jungman, the movement was an attempt to return Christianity to the basics of the early church — that is to say, proclaiming the gospel. Its goal, as one report stressed, was "to present the truth of our faith as an organic whole. Its core [was] the good news of our redemption in Christ. Its fruit [was to] be the grateful response of our love." Because its focus was on Christ, it became known as Christocentric. The kerygmatic movement stressed, however, that there was a "fourfold presentation" to be given to the faithful: liturgy, scriptures, systematic teaching, and the example of Christian living were all to be part of the package. It was supposed to be a lively change from the supposedly dull and rote practices of learning the catechism.

The kerygmatic approach, however, soon became something rather different from what its originators intended. The trouble was evident in 1962, during the International Catechetical Study Week. The ICS Weeks were gatherings of clergy and educators, and their purpose was to examine teaching in terms of missionary work. However, the ICS Week had a tremendous influence on Catholic teaching in general. At the 1960 ICS Week the subject was the kerygmatic movement, and the stated aims were nothing that would upset Pat Buchanan — or John Paul II, who was a strong supporter of the movement. The 1960 conference emphasized the four aspects of teaching the faith — liturgy, Bible, systematic teaching, and the example of Christian living.

At the third Study Week, held in 1962, a strange concept slipped into the idea of mission catechesis. The emphasis was not only on developing "a fuller response to the doctrine of Christ," but also "special emphasis on adaption by developing the doctrine according to analogies, images, or forms of expression familiar to people of a given religion or culture." As Msgr. Michael Wrenn notes in his book *Catechisms and Controversies*, "It cannot be repeated too often that the faith is something that was 'delivered once and for all to the saints' (Jude 3) and has never in the church's tradition been considered something to be adapted but rather something to be handed down intact."

The 1962 ICS Week represented a major shift, from focus on God to focus on man. A key aspect of the kerygmatic movement was now "pre-evangelization," or concentrating on the nature of man and his particular political or cultural circumstances. It was, in short, anthropocentric. By the late 1960s the ICS Week and the kerygmatic movement completely lost their Christocentric nature. At the ICS Week in 1967, for example, Christ almost seemed beside the point. In fact, the gathering called the church "a ghetto group that seemed more concerned with the defense of its privileges than the building up of the human community [and] little committed to social reform and to the struggle for social justice." This was the germ of liberation theology, the pro-Marxist form of Christianity that would infect the church, particularly the Jesuits, in the 1980s.

Although Catholic University, like the new catechism movement, had been a home to radicals even before Vatican II, the dissent came to the forefront on July 25, 1968. On that day Pope Paul IV issued his encyclical *Humanae Vitae* affirming the church's teaching that the "rhythm" method of regulating births was the only appropriate form of birth control for Catholics. Anger at his decision was widespread among liberal clergy and was so intense at Catholic University that nineteen openly dissatisfied priests were disciplined by Cardinal Patrick O'Boyle.

Although *Humanae Vitae* is often cited as a dividing point in the church's history, it's more important to understand that the slow erosion of faith over the last forty years could not have taken place had

Catholic teachers not abandoned the catechism. The trouble had taken root even before Vatican II, but after the council the dissent in the church became overt. In 1966 the Dutch bishops issued *A New Catechism*, which was widely praised by liberal Catholics. The Dutch catechism reflected a "new theology," which basically meant that Catholics were no longer required to follow the magisterium in terms of what to believe or teach. Pope Paul VI assigned a commission to examine the Dutch catechism, and the commission identified ten doctrinal errors in the document. The recommended corrections were never made; they were simply added as an appendix.

Soon other volumes appeared that reflected more the liberal 1960s than the Vatican. One of the most popular and most typical was the book *Christ Among Us* by Anthony Wilhelm. Wilhelm didn't hedge about his view: "It might well be an overly audacious, even foolhardy attempt to speak about God and his revelation at a time when Christianity is undergoing a universal questioning and theology a massive reconstruction.... Today nothing is more apparent than that we know very little indeed."

> *Yet a central problem of the education crisis in the church stems from the fact that books like* Christ Among Us *were taught in the schools and celebrated in the Catholic press.*

Wilhelm's trick was not to deny the actual structure of the church or the rules, but to attempt to devastate them with relentless and subversive commentary. Examples abound. Wilhelm refers to infallibility and then offers up this sentence: "By its infallibility, the Church does not claim to possess the whole truth of God and his relationship to man, but only what we humans are able to see of his revelation at this particular point in history." Just for good measure, Wilhelm adds that, "Actually, the Church's infallible teachings, which give us a measure of certainty in our service of God, say very little." Wilhelm also manages to take authority away from Peter, the rock on which

Christ founded the church. "Peter went eventually to Rome, where his position as leader of the early Christian Church was passed on to his successors, the bishops of Rome. Peter's leadership is evident in the early church, yet not as one endowed with supreme jurisdiction; all the apostles had been commissioned by Christ and evidently felt little need to defer to Peter."

Wilhelm's biggest whopper involved the Resurrection itself. To Wilhelm, the Resurrection occurred only to those who believed. "To believe in Christ's divinity one must have an open mind and a willingness to live his teachings — and the power of faith. Skeptics, those whose minds are closed to His teachings or to moral improvement, like Herod, Pontius Pilate, and the Pharisees, probably would have seen nothing had they been with the Apostles when Christ appeared after his Resurrection." He seems to be saying that the Resurrection was a delusion or wishful thinking.

Christ Among Us also has several examples of bland, narcissistic blather that became popular in the 1960s. "Each person's soul is a special 'aspect' of God's continuing creation of the universe — an individual spiritual power that comes about by the evolutionary process which God began, working out itself in each of us." Or — "God's grace-presence gives us the power to transform everything we do into eternal happiness for ourselves and others. . . . God's plan was that man would develop so that he could have his grace-presence, grow in it, and be with Him forever in heaven. He would send His Son, Jesus Christ, to earth when men were ready, to fill us with a superabundance of this grace-presence." According to Wilhelm, "The universe is now 'in labor' towards [a] better state. . . . It is up to us to bring about this new universe."

This kind of stuff would be merely annoying if it were considered fringe theology by the majority of Catholics. Yet a central problem of the education crisis in the church stems from the fact that books like *Christ Among Us* were taught in the schools and celebrated in the Catholic press. After *Christ Among Us* had been used as a textbook for over ten years, it finally dawned on Rome that the things that Wilhelm wrote might not square with the magisterium. The Congregation for the Doctrine of the Faith requested that Wilhelm's book have its imprimatur removed. The Archdiocese of Newark complied, but none of this slowed the book's use and popularity. Harper & Row immediately published *Christ Among Us* without its imprimatur. In 1990, an ad in the Catholic magazine *Commonweal* called *Christ Among Us* "today's most widely read introduction to Catholicism." The *New York Times* called the book "the nation's most widely used introduction to Catholicism." The Catholic News Service praised *Christ Among Us* as "a fine piece of scholarship." It has sold over a million copies.

Another popular figure in catechism who was indicative of the time was Brother Gabriel Moran. In a 1970 *Commonweal* article, "Catechetics, R.I.P.," Moran announced that "anyone who sets out to educate in the field of religion has to put scripture, liturgy, and Christian theology in a broader context that does not afford Christianity a normative role." Moran complained of "right-wingers" in the church who were wasting "their energies searching out heresy at a time when that problem has been swallowed up by the much larger question of the existence of any Christianity at all."

Moran, an "acknowledged expert" in the religious education of Catholics, apparently didn't think there were any Catholics left and that truth was impossible to define. You would think that such a philosophy would make someone a poor candidate for teaching the catechism, but in the 1980s Moran was asked to revise and expand "Catechetics, R.I.P." for inclusion in the *Sourcebook for Modern Catechetics*. Msgr. Michael J. Wrenn was incredulous. "Can this be right?" he wrote. "An author repudiates Christianity itself, yet not only goes on considering himself a Catholic religious educator but continues to be considered by others as well, to the point that he is included as a contributor in a comprehensive anthology on the subject published over a decade after his repudiation of Christianity."

In the feverish, anti-establishment atmosphere of the 1960s and 1970s, none of this was strange at all. The *General Catechetical Directory* of 1971 noted that there was a problem not just outside but within the church itself. The GCD spoke of "errors which are not infrequently noted in catechetics today." The only way to avoid most errors was for those teaching it to "start with the correct way of understanding the nature and purpose of catechism and also the truths which are to be taught by it." There was little chance of that. In 1972, a year after the publication of the GCD, the National Conference of Diocesan Directors of Religious Education declined to "receive" the document. The NCDDRE issued its own "commentary" on the GCD called *Focus on American Catechetics*. *Focus* and the NCDDRE were affiliated with the National Catholic Education Association. *Focus* subverted the message of the GCD, often by seeming to agree with it. For example, *Focus* agrees with GCD's assertion that faith is a gift of God and that in this gift man receives divine revelation. Then *Focus* adds its own spin, claiming that there are two types of revelation — the old fashioned kind, which saw it as a gift from God, and the new kind. *Focus* elaborates:

> On the other hand, if the educator views revelation in more dramatic and personal terms, he will seek to become conscious of the signs of the living God present in their own lives. He will not see his task as primarily transmitting unspoiled doctrines from the deep freeze of the past, but rather as helping the student reflect on his own experience. He will begin from the experience of the student and will provide real and vicarious experiences upon which the student can reflect.

Thus the focus of religious faith moves from God to the student — and to the changing culture. According to *Focus*, "Catechetical problems which are blind to the inevitability of ongoing change in society in general and the Church in particular can only tragically retard the religious development of students who must live in the world of tomorrow."

How different this was from the ethos of Chesterton, Maritain, and the other members of the great Catholic intellectual Renaissance of the early twentieth century. These intellectuals were modern men, but only insofar as modernism could express the timeless truths of Catholicism. Maritain praised democracy, but only as long as it was grounded in natural law. Etienne Gilson praised abstract expressionism, but only as a creative expression whose driving force was God. To be honest, Chesterton and other creative people were often shunned in the church. To too many on the Right, Christianity was a warm, comfortable, never-changing set of beliefs that don't call for revolutionary action — or even much creativity. Yet the far left ideas of liberation theology, the Marxist worldview that was already bubbling in the church in the 1960s, also lacked any idea of genuine Christian humanism. The problem with both worldviews was explored in an article Thomas Merton wrote in 1967 in *Spiritual Life*, a charming quarterly published by the Washington Province of Discalced Carmelite Friars. The essay, "Christian Humanism," is a cogent exploration of Christian humanism, which in the febrile, antiauthoritarian, and skeptical atmosphere of the 1960s — an atmosphere still very much with us — was considered an oxymoron. To the secular culture, observes Merton, religion "diminishes man's human stature, blunts his creativity, and retards his growth towards maturity."

Merton observes that by the 1960s, Christianity itself had failed to convey its truly radical nature. It had offered the world a vision of existence where "the only function of man's freedom is to discover and accept what has already been imposed upon him by God without any consideration for his own creative possibilities." Indeed, Christianity to many seemed ahistorical, when in fact Christianity "can not only throw light on the most typical and urgent problems of the modern world, but there is a certain light which Christianity alone can provide." This was through Christian love, which had been sentimentalized and formalized, but in reality was a revolutionary, ever-new, creative, and world-changing force — that is, it could be so if based on genuine selfless love, forgiveness, and, more than anything else, on following Christ. Through such love one could feed the poor, transform a racist society, end wars, create great art, and give the down-and-out a sense of worth and responsibility.

This is the great paradox of Christianity, that by strictly following the teachings of Christ one can experience an explosion of freedom and creativity — and a creativity that has no end. Christian humanism says that God both knows our lives beginning to end and can still delight when we make something new and beautiful, whether a poem, piece of music, painting, or film. Sadly, many Christian conservatives

won't accept this, only reading books and seeing films that bolster
their faith in the simplest, most bland way — the *Left Behind* series
and Christian rock. Robust Christians can see the gospel proclaimed
not only in the Bible — and in the White House — but in popular
culture. The music of U2 proclaims it. Films — even popcorn ones
such as *The X-Men* — preach it. Jonathan Franzen's bestseller *The
Corrections* had reoccurring and compelling references to Aslan, the
lion who was a Christ figure in C. S. Lewis's *Narnia* books. Yet many
in red-state America consider this heathen stuff. No wonder so many
in the arts think Christianity is a stagnant religion. It's not stagnant,
but many of its salespeople are. On the Right, there is suspicion of
art — particularly popular art — and anti-intellectualism. On the
Left, the problem of misinterpreting and limiting Christianity has
led to the abstraction of Marxism. To many, it is humanity, not
religion, that will usher in the utopia of genuine humanism. It's a
grand vision, but one, as Merton noted, that "had little patience for
the claims of the fallible human person and no interest whatever in
such values as love, compassion, mercy, happiness." This explains
in part why, wrote Merton, "modern secular humanisms are so fair
and optimistic in theory and so utterly merciless and inhuman in
practice. It is very easy to complacently love abstract humanity as
the idolatrous projection of self while hating mercilessly my concrete
fellow man."

To the contributors of *Focus*, the equation had been reversed: the
gospel didn't reflect wisdom that was ever ancient and ever new; it
was a historically questionable story that could only with difficulty
fit the problems of the modern age. Indeed, those cited by *Focus*
read like a who's who of dissenters from the magisterium. Writing
about how sin is actually different from what the GCD said was
Father Charles F. Curran, a dissenter who was fired from teaching at
Catholic University when I was a student there in the 1980s. Gregory
Baum is the authority on revelation — the same Gregory Baum who
wrote:

> The manner of thinking and speaking about God in traditional
> Christian piety, and even in most professional theology, is no

longer in harmony with the contemporary experience of reality. What is wrong, for today, in the traditional manner is the objectification of God. Because of the change in the understanding of man and his world, it has become impossible to think of God as a being over and above human history.

Other dissenters who were cited as authorities were John Dedek and Richard P. McBrien. As Michael J. Wrenn observes, this view often meant "a systematic professional formation that included indoctrination in current anti-Church and anti-magisterium positions and attitudes — not to speak of growing disdain for the humble task of trying to pass on the inherited message at all."

Wrenn also noted that this view often meant subverting the catechism through books. In 1973 the National Conference of Catholic Bishops released the document *Basic Teachings for Catholic Religious Education*. It was intended to correct some of the abuses that were going on in Catholic education. In response, the Division of Religious Education–CCD of the United States Catholic Conference issued its own booklet, *A Study Aid for Basic Teachings for Catholic Religious Education*. The study aid recommended eighty-two books for classroom use by religious educators. Many of the books flatly contradicted the guidelines that had been recommended in the Basic Teachings. One book, *New Horizon: Theological Essays*, included the Baum words noted above. Another book, *The God of Space and Time*, announced that "Christian faith is not the acceptance of a body of doctrines nor is it the observance of laws or the performance of a cult." Yet another, *How Do I Know I'm Doing Right?*, declared that "Seeking moral guidance through our Roman Catholic Church alone is an appeal which we are not wise to make in any Christian matter, doctrinal or moral." Perhaps most outrageous was this claim, made in *God, Jesus, and Spirit*: "Christ does not supply any ready-made answers for the questions of contemporary men. His life is not proposed as an answer to the questions which man's being presupposes. He gives no revealed doctrines about God nor any revealed precepts for leading a proper life."

This assault on the church was pushed along by church liberals and the media — not only the mainstream media but also the Catholic media. The major anti-Catholic weapon in the secular media was John Cogley. Cogley was a radical Catholic who in 1965 was named the religious news editor of the *New York Times*. Vatican II was in its fourth and final year, and there were dissenting voices in the church calling for the end of the proscription of contraception. The church would not change its teaching, however, and in 1968 Pope Paul VI issued *Humanae Vitae,* defending its position.

Cogley would eventually confess that he had left the church in the early 1960s. He was a foreshadowing of the twenty-first-century Catholic journalist — people like E. J. Dionne and Andrew Sullivan — who claim to be Catholic yet attack some of the church's most fundamental beliefs. (We will turn our attention to them later.) Cogley was an ardent supporter of contraception, and *Humanae Vitae* would ultimately drive him (in 1973) to become an Episcopalian. Reading Cogley's dispatches from the mid-1960s is actually amusing, not dissimilar to perusing the reports in the *Times* filed in the 1930s by its Russian correspondent Walter Duranty, who claimed that there was no starvation or repression in Stalin's Soviet Union. Duranty was a piker compared to Cogley, who in 1966 gave a speech that obliterated the line separating advocacy from hysterical, fanatical zeal.

Cogley's major article about birth control and Catholicism appeared on June 20, 1965, as a lengthy piece in the *New York Times Magazine.* He starts the piece with an old joke — the one about the priest who meets a man in a hospital waiting room who is expecting his sixth child. The priest praises the man, only to call him a "sex addict" when he learns he's not Catholic. "Some council fathers will admit...that the church may be in a bind [over contraception]," Cogley announces. He then notes that Catholics "in various parts of the country have banded together" to make sure that contraception is not accepted by certain state and federal employees. These Catholics are not interviewed. There are, however, lengthy quotes from dissenters — from the director of the Family Life Bureau of the National Catholic Welfare Conference to the Reverend John Courtney Murray, a favorite of liberal reporters.

Cogley declares that "even some more conservative theologians have now let it be known that they believe that with the development of modern anovulents — or 'The Pill,' as it is called in an upper-case tone of voice at informal clerical gatherings — the church has been providentially presented with a graceful 'way out.'" Cogley quotes only one theologian who stands against birth control, but he is barely audible amid the scores of voices in the five-page piece who cry out for change. Unfortunately, some of these enlightened folks are afraid to speak because of the big bad church. Indeed, this fear provides one of the money quotes in Cogley's piece:

> The present position of the church, they will tell you bluntly if you promise not to quote them, is sown with ambiguities and contradictions. The more the church insists, they say, the more Catholics with all the goodwill in the world are cut off from its rich sacramental life. The more earnestly many young couples try to live up to such a position, the more they find themselves drifting apart emotionally.... The more obedience couples give to the present Catholic understanding of the natural law, the more "unnaturally" they are required to behave as semi-celibates sharing the same bed. Frequently, the more children a couple have, the less satisfying and enriching their love life, and the less able they are to live up to their moral obligations as parents.

Cogley's article was just part of a larger movement in the media of the time to push the church into overturning its guidelines on contraception. *Time, Newsweek,* and *U.S. News and World Report* all ran slanted stories about the "controversy" within the Catholic Church, despite the fact that most theologians and bishops supported the ban on contraception. In 1965 and 1966 *Look* magazine published three articles whose titles gave the game away: "The Catholic Revolution," "Lady Doctor Defies Her Church," and "The Pope's Unsolvable Problem." In April 1964 the *Saturday Evening Post* published feminist Rosemary Ruether's "A Catholic Mother Tells Why 'I Believe in Birth Control.'" In it she announced that the rhythm method "does great psychological damage." In July 1965 *Redbook* published a piece called "This Baby Will Be My Last." And so on.

In fact, the media was actually creating the conditions for dissent and would then report on that dissent as a fact of life. This was pointed out by James Hitchcock: "The key concept was that of supposed 'trends' that were developing and which the press was merely reporting. To establish such trends, however, it was necessary either to ignore all evidence against them" — and here Hitchcock notes that most theologians and bishops in 1965 supported the traditional teaching on contraception — or "treat it as unimportant. The postulation of a trend... was at best a guess on the part of the reporters, rendered all the more dubious by the obvious desire of most of the press that such a change should take place."

Cogley's high point of lunacy, and a rhetorical high point of dour modern Catholicism, came in August 1966, when he addressed the National Catholic Education Association. Cogley's lecture was so hectoring, didactic, and virulently tendentious against the church that it actually elicits a kind of perverse admiration. The man could not have cared less that he was supposed to be the religious news editor of the *New York Times* and therefore, one might suppose, somewhat objective. His bravado is bracing, if idiotic. "We Catholics, thank God, have burned our last heretic," he exults. "Let us hope the time is not far off when we will have excommunicated our last sinner, anathemized our last dissenter, and perhaps even suspended our last rebellious priest."

Cogley constantly refers to the Second Vatican Council as "revolutionary," noting the irony of this sea change being brought about by the traditional leaders of the church: "There were men among the Founding Fathers of this nation who could not foresee the full implications of their own soaring words about human equality, liberty, and justice toward all. Similarly, among the council fathers, there were some who apparently did not realize that by opening the doors they were permitting the future to walk in with bold steps." As for those "conservatives" who would attempt to stem this tide of change, Cogley predicts — or rather, guarantees — that when the

church tells its followers that Vatican II didn't change anything fundamental about Catholicism, "the religious news columns will belie
all the assumptions." He would certainly be one person to make sure
of that.

By 1970, when I was entering Our Lady of Mercy for the first
grade, the transformation of Catholic life and education was virtually
complete. Nails Herlihy was gone, a vestige of a former age, and
modern giants like Chesterton had been forgotten. Catholic kids were
now in the hands of good liberals who would teach them their own
catechism — the catechism of lax morals and hostility to the church.
The *National Catholic Reporter* acknowledged as much in an article
in 1971:

> It is simply true that the religion texts of today are vastly differ-
> ent from those of yesteryear, that progressivist views dominate
> most Catholic religious and theological training, that in conse-
> quence the Catholicism of tomorrow will be something new on
> earth — and that all this has been accomplished in something
> less than democratic fashion, by ways and means that eluded
> standard ecclesiastical safeguards. There is a liberal conspir-
> acy: liberal theologians dominate the public prints [press], the
> catechetical training centers, the publishing houses, the profes-
> sional associations, much of Catholic bureaucracy; they praise
> each other's books, award each other contracts, jobs, and pre-
> requisites. I doubt that the kids are getting even a sympathetic
> explanation of what their parents used to believe, much less an
> option to choose between old-style and new-style Catholicism.
> Indoctrination is anathema to liberals on principle; but there
> are ways and ways of indoctrinating.

I would, however, get a taste of old school Catholicism. In 1971
my teacher was Sister Stephanie, who was, at least in part, the em-
bodiment of the pre–Vatican II Catholic nun. Gruff, no-nonsense,
and often mean, Stephanie still wore the traditional habit despite
Rome's 1965 decree that clergy could wear more moderate clothing.

Sister Stephanie had a husky build, a face so pallid it seemed as if
blood hadn't circulated through her body in years, and the cat-eyed

glasses that had been popular in the 1950s and 1960s. We sat in the classroom while she drilled into us the alphabet, discipline, and the catechism of the Catholic Church. We learned about hell, purgatory, offering our own suffering up for other souls, and the boundless love of God. Sister Stephanie marked our papers with angel stamps, bold black-and-white ink representations of God's winged messengers.

I still vividly remember those angels, not because they represented something comfortable and fake, but for the opposite reason: they were images of something that I knew in my soul was real. Sister Stephanie reminded us that angels were more than just cute. She agreed with what Josef Pieper had written: "An angel is a being of such superior keenness of intellect and such penetrating brilliance of mind that we should consider him awesome rather than charming or pretty. By essence, angels are not the playthings of little children. . . . Such a concept is not without beauty in its symbolic emphasis on the purity of the angels, but it does not reach the essential greatness of the angels."

Sister Stephanie was an anachronism, someone who had grown up in the harvest years of American Catholicism. She believed it was more important to cross yourself if you passed a church or bow your head in silent contemplation at three o'clock on Good Friday, the time of Christ's death, than to be current with the latest trends and diversions of the modern world. She believed in teaching the catechism, and she would be one of the few teachers I had in Catholic school who held that conviction. She believed in the greatness of God, and that if we ever charted the known universe we would not even begin to comprehend God.

After I had Sister Stephanie in the first grade, my religious education effectively ended. In the post–Vatican II world the *Baltimore Catechism* was out, and the *General Catechetical Directory* was not being used. In 1972 Cardinal John J. Wright, the man who in 1955 had lamented the anti-intellectualism in the church, now announced a crisis in Catholic teaching. He defended the old way of learning the faith, i.e., through memorization, and insisted that the modern problems stemmed from the tangle of modern theology, which obscured faith behind a thicket of theory. He singled out an article

called "Toward a Theology of Hope": "After 2,000 years since Cal-
vary, what in the name of heaven does that title mean? Toward a
Theology of Hope! Toward a Theology of Community — 2,000 years
after the Cenacle and the Last Supper! Toward a theology of this,
and toward a theology of that — they are all what they call searching. All this means is that in the crisis of faith they have lost their
way and they thumb a ride from any guy driving along." Wright attacked the attackers of the old school of catechesis — the people who
called it brainwashing and demanded a new form of teaching, based
on self-expression, that would be done "in the spirit of the council,"
meaning Vatican II. "Never mind the letter of the Council," Wright
said. "Most of the people who talk to me about the spirit of the
Council haven't read a paragraph of the documents of the Council.
So there isn't much talk about the letter of the Council, but a lot of
talk about the spirit, and out of this has come this confusion of the
purely subjective and pluralistic and personalistic and individualistic
nature of the Faith which is one: one Lord, one Faith, one baptism."
He noted that others have encouraged the church to publish a syllabus of errors. The problem, Wright announced, was that such a
book would be as long as the *Encyclopaedia Britannica.*

At Our Lady of Mercy, we didn't have bad religious education, we
had no religious education. Oh, we went to Mass, but had no idea
what we were looking at. We received the sacraments — confession,
confirmation, Holy Communion — but didn't know what they meant.
Mass was mandatory, but (unlike when my older brothers had gone
to Mercy in the 1960s) being an altar boy was not. It had become
optional, and I had opted out. I couldn't name the disciples, never
mind any saints. I was a Catholic illiterate kept that way in a Catholic
school.

It was almost as if our teachers did not want us to learn our faith —
or even to think about God at all. I remember a particular afternoon
in 1976. I was twelve years old and in sixth grade at Our Lady of
Mercy. On this particular afternoon Mr. Sowell, our teacher, was
trying to teach us social studies, a course suffused with proto-PC
claims about the "values of all cultures" and other nonsense.

The class wanted no part of it. A few days before, Mr. Sowell had made the mistake of playing the class a tape of a young and intensely charismatic preacher. I forget the man's name, but he was the most electrifying speaker I had ever heard. He had been a drug addict, dope dealer, and thief, but had discovered the Lord and was set right. He had a staccato delivery, and an assurance born of faith, that were riveting. One part that I never forgot was when his life was bottoming out and he was arrested. He had prayed for the first time in his life the night before, and when he tried to mouth off to the police he couldn't speak. Then he tried to take a swing but couldn't move his hand. "I didn't realize it at the time," he said, "but I was caught. An angel held my tongue, and another held my arm."

We cried out with delight. We had been born in the 1960s, and many of our older brothers (although not mine) and their friends were hippies. The culture was increasingly telling us that the highest aspiration of man was to feel good and buy things — after all, we lived in one of the wealthiest suburbs of Washington. This preacher was telling us that the pot some of our older brothers smoked was poison, and that material things meant nothing. I never forgot the image of two winged messengers restraining this man, clutching his filthy denim arm (it was the 1970s, so the bad guys in my mind were hippies) and rancid, pot-soaked tongue. The class was mesmerized, girls turning their heads in attention, boys leaning forward to catch every word. After that, it was hard for Mr. Sowell to teach social studies. Now we were hungry for God. He did play us one more tape of the preacher, but that was it.

Mr. Sowell, like every one of my teachers at Mercy after Sister Stephanie, was not a member of any religious order. The only priests we saw were Father Gatto, a tough, middle-aged Italian priest who ran the parish, and his assistant, a young, skinny man named Father Brennan. Father Brennan gave what amounted to religion class. About once every few weeks he would stop by the classroom and entertain questions we may have had about God. Since we hadn't been taught anything, we didn't have much to ask. Most of the questions were of the dumb "How much do angels weigh?" variety.

Father Gatto, however, was from old-school Catholicism, a man not dissimilar to Nails Herlihy, the terror of Gonzaga in the 1940s. Father Gatto always looked immaculate, as if he had just prepared himself to win an award. His coal-black hair was tightly combed back and held in place with gel. His priestly smock was dust free. He stood straight and exuded physical power, like a boxer. He would come to the classroom on report card day and hand out our cards. It was often a humiliating experience — at least for those of us who weren't the serious students we should have been. Father Gatto would announce the name and then, while the student took the long walk to the front of the class, would comment on the grades. The goody-goodies and brainiacs always got encouragement — "Very good, Paul! You're especially strong in science. But let's try to bring those PE marks up."

Then they would come to me. The teacher called my name, and the walk of shame began. "You've got to do some improving, young man!" Gatto would blast as I struggled to make the twenty feet to the front of the room. "A C in chemistry, what's that all about? Disciplinary problems, what's going on there! You're going to have to shape up!"

These days I could probably sue a teacher for doing the same thing to a kid, but Gatto was right. I was an underachiever, or maybe I had ADD.

Father Gatto was our first confessor and the main priest who said mass and did the stations of the cross on Good Friday. When he did the stations of the cross, majestically striding through the markers of Christ's final agony, the church seemed like an opera house. His voice filled every space. Trailing him were the altar boys. Shortly after I arrived, Mercy made being an altar boy optional. I was the first one in the school's history to opt out. I still remember telling Father Gatto. It was on a rainy day, and I was on the sidewalk outside the school walking to class. Gatto appeared out of the side door of the church and cut me off. Altar boy practice had been the night before — where was I? "I quit," I stammered. I actually had not quit, since I never joined. Nonetheless, his tough Italian face pinched into a frown. He took his umbrella and jabbed it right in between my legs. "You quit?" he cried. "Well, that's just awful." He was angry but also seemed deeply hurt. The order to let boys decide whether to join or not had come from higher-ups, and he could do nothing about it. He probably thought he was potentially losing a soul. He was right. Probably my single biggest disappointment at Mercy was when they stopped showing the classic 1950s movie *Our Lady of Fatima*. Every spring as the school year was coming to a close the students would congregate in the cafeteria — called the Kennedy Room — and watch the movie. For years, my most visceral connection to Catholicism wasn't in class, or even in mandatory Mass, but in that movie. At the end, when the sun came close to the earth and all the pilgrims began freaking out, it seemed to me as real as Father Gatto's starched collar. This miracle had happened.

Our Lady of Fatima was a spring tradition at Mercy dating back to the school's founding in the early 1960s. But suddenly — I remember it being around the time I was in third grade — they just stopped showing it. It was shortly after that the rules for the way nuns dress were changed. Sister Stephanie retired, but the principal of the school, an energetic and kind nun named Sister Elaine, suddenly appeared one day without her habit. She wore a modern blue dress that didn't seem to have any noticeable religious symbols.

Suddenly it was hard to tell the difference between the nuns and the mothers. This made for those awkward moments, which happened to me throughout my entire Catholic education, where you would be talking to a woman for ten minutes before figuring out she was a nun. In one disastrous episode in college, I was at a party and went on a profanity-spewing rant about how much some band sucked, only to have the young lady I was trying to impress give me a blank look. She was a nun.

The change in dress was an indication that to many religious, and the Catholic laity, being worldly was more important than being a visible representative of Christ. Still, it's hard to say whether properly attired nuns and a more compelling and orthodox Catholic education would have helped me at this point. I may have suffered from what the church calls "invincible ignorance" no matter what. My dad once said, "You were rebelling when you came outta your mom," and he was probably right. I just had an instinct and desire to get into trouble, and science and psychotherapy are useless to explain it. I just liked causing trouble. At Mercy, this took the form of many afternoons in detention, and, as Father Gatto knew, some bad grades. Still, perhaps it would have done some good to have learned about St. Augustine or Thomas Merton, two Catholics who had also been rebellious as young men. As it was, to me the only cool thing about the church was the way the sun danced at Fatima. I guess it was better than nothing. For his part, my dad figured if he just kept feeding me books I would make it through somehow. It would have helped if the church had put a man like Father Gatto in the classroom instead of having him running the school bureaucracy.

All throughout Mercy — and indeed later at Prep and Catholic University — my main connection to the richness of Catholicism was my father. Unlike my teachers, Dad knew a basic truth of the faith: that the supernatural world exists. This idea used to be frequently emphasized in Catholic catechism and literature. In his 1952 book *The Faith in Action,* the Reverend Francis J. Mueller dedicated an entire chapter to the idea that "the supernatural is superior." "By his faith," Mueller wrote, "the Christian has a foot in each of two worlds. He is a citizen of two cities, the visible and the invisible, the natural and the supernatural, and the visible is the less real." Mueller insisted that "the Catholic has better reason to be certain about the facts of revelation than he has about what his eyes can comprehend. Eyes may be misled; faith can't be. All of which reduces to just this single bald fact: revelation provides a greater certitude than experience."

I learned this, not at school, but from my dad. To my dad, the world itself was enchanted, filled with wonder and poetry — with what Aldous Huxley called "the monster of the obvious." I remember that my father loved Halloween but became increasingly irritated as the holiday became safer and more commercialized. To him, Halloween wasn't about "a bunch of little farts running around in costume" but a portal into a frightening pagan world of the dead. The Mass was literally the transformation of bread and wine into the body and blood of Jesus Christ. Literally. While the Catholic schools had stopped teaching Catholicism, I was catechized by my dad in the books he insisted we all read: *The Chronicles of Narnia* by C. S. Lewis, Tolkien's *The Lord of the Rings*, Ursula K. Le Guin's "Earthsea Cycle," Catholic novelist Charles Williams's *All Hallows Eve*. He understood that these so-called works of fantasy opened a door to a reality, the reality of God, that was as real as — indeed, more real than — the air that we were breathing.

Sadly, my teachers at Mercy were impressed with my father not as a Catholic, but as a journalist and editor at *National Geographic*, even though his stories reflected his faith. In 1972 he wrote a remarkable article about Israel, recounting his camel ride to the top of Mt. Sinai. And a few years later he profiled Boston. In that piece he described the Society of St. Anthony, which every year carried a statue of the great saint around the neighborhood as a reminder of the faith. "The saint gave them the blessing they sought," Dad wrote. "The security of a united people, an identity in a hard industrial world, a reminder of who they really were."

At Mercy, we were taught to forget.

– *Chapter Four* –

Prep

In 1979 the church issued *Sharing the Light of Faith: National Cate-chetical Directory for Catholics of the United States.* The document had been assembled by the American bishops and examined for over a year by several Roman congregations. As with the *General Catechet-ical Directory,* the document was not implemented by the American religious establishment. The National Conference of Diocesan Di-rectors of Religious Education (NCDDRE) published its *Discussion Guide to Sharing the Light of Faith.* It flatly contradicted *Sharing* on an abundance of points, including the existence of original sin. Its au-thor was Father Thomas Sullivan, who had written *Focus on American Catechetics.* The Department of Education of the U.S. Catholic Con-ference devoted a special issue of its religious journal, *The Living Light,* to *Sharing.* In the foreword, Father Sullivan states that "the Church in our day is not . . . of one mind in all things, and the *Directory* under-standably reflects some of the ambiguity of the current scene." Sister Anne Marie Mongoven announced that "the Directory reflects our diversity and unity. . . . Every reader can look and find whatever he or she wants to see." In response, the U.S. Catholic Conference pub-lished *An Introduction to Sharing the Light of Faith.* Msgr. George A. Kelly of St. John's University identified at least twelve major errors in the *Living Light* issue on key matters such as sin, conscience, moral-ity, infallibility, and birth control. Indeed the *Introduction* went so far as to refer to "the Church's teaching concerning moral methods of regulating births."

All of this was too much for the Reverend Alfred McBride, who worked at the NCEA (National Catholic Education Association) at the time. In 1992, some thirteen years later, he reflected back on the collapse of Catholic education:

> The chaos in religious education today has resulted from an agenda that pretended to implement Vatican II, but in fact subverted it.... Over a period of twenty-five years, [certain theologians and catechetical writers] gained influence and control of the departments of religion and religious education in Catholic colleges and universities, of the publishers of the most widely-used religion textbooks, and of the middle management positions and archdioceses. They were and are the major speakers at most religious education conventions. Through their books and articles and classroom indoctrination, they shape the minds of the leaders, who in turn pass this on to the classroom and volunteer teachers. They are not teaching Catholicism but rather a mélange of personal opinions that usually resurrect discredited nineteenth-century liberal Protestantism and reflect New Age pieties. Bad theory had led to bad practice.

Things did not get better when I left Mercy. I went to Georgetown Prep, a famous all-boys Jesuit school in Maryland. Although Georgetown Prep has a golden reputation as a Catholic school, it was actually anything but Catholic by the time I got there in the 1980s. The school was run by Jesuits who, like the members of the catechetical elite, had become hostile to the church since at least 1960. The Jesuits had been founded by Ignatius Loyola and for most of their four hundred plus years had earned their reputation as "The Pope's marines," traveling around the world setting up schools and preaching the gospel. This changed in the 1960s. The effect of Vatican II, a new interest in therapy, enchantment with the youth culture, and even the physical location of Jesuit seminaries, all combined to undermine the Jesuits.

The transformation of the Jesuits has been documented in books such as Malachi Martin's *The Jesuits* and James Hitchcock's *The Pope and the Jesuits*. A couple of examples will help us to understand the atmosphere at Georgetown Prep. One of the strongest and most respected Jesuit seminaries was the Woodstock Theologate in

Maryland, founded in 1869. Whereas it was once held that having a seminary in the countryside would help foster prayer, study, and religious contemplation among the novices, in 1969 the Jesuits decided that Woodstock would do better to join the modern world. It was moved to Morningside Heights in New York City, near Columbia University. The Jesuit residences would not be at a central location, but in a group of apartments at five locations along Manhattan's Upper West Side. As Malachi Martin observes, these apartments soon became "crash pads," home to unorthodox liturgy parties and even dates. Father Walter Burghardt, editor of the Jesuit *Theological Review,* claimed that "experimentation with different lifestyles is indispensable for our Jesuit students if we are to prepare for a contemporary ministry." The relocation of Woodstock was an absolute failure. Edward Sponga, the Jesuit provincial who orchestrated the move, left the society to marry his secretary. After a few years the school closed but would reappear in 1974 at Georgetown University. It would be the stage for an open rebellion against a new catechism of the Catholic Church published in 1992.

Woodstock has also produced John J. McNeil, a theologian who in 1976 published *The Church and the Homosexual,* which was the culmination of years McNeil had spent trying to legitimize homosexuality. Although McNeil's book passed Jesuit censors, he was silenced by the Vatican. Several Jesuits, including the famous radical Daniel Berrigan, came to McNeil's defense. In a sense, they had a point: there were many other Jesuits openly advocating homosexuality who were not silenced by the church. Peter Fink, theologian at Weston, a Jesuit training school near Boston, had proposed that the Catholic Church "explore the hypothesis" that homosexuality was valid. Fink's Weston colleague Edward Vacek had promoted a similar idea. They had plenty of company. In 1977 a group of Jesuits signed a petition sponsored by the Catholic Coalition for Gay Civil Rights. In 1974 twenty-eight of the Jesuits at Woodstock attacked the Archdiocese of New York for opposing a gay rights bill in the city council. In 1977 Jesuit George Casey was implicated in an incident in which a gay rights group struck the archbishop of Minneapolis with a pie because of his opposition to gay rights.

What had gone wrong? In *The Jesuits*, Martin traces the problem back to modernism and the influence of dissident Jesuits, most notably Pierre Teilhard de Chardin. Modernism, which had begun in the late nineteenth century, can be summarized as an assault on orthodox religion from those who believe that human reason and science would lead to greater human happiness than the old superstitions. Modernists might be materialists and atheists, and they might subscribe to a form of spirituality that had more to do with gnosticism than with the discovery of a new set of timeless truths.

Martin notes the impact of the Hindu monk Swami Vivekananda at the 1893 World's Parliament of Religions in Chicago. The swami, Martin observes, made his sappy spiritual bromides "fit . . . remarkably well with the journey of science and humanism toward a new idea of material perfection." One of the swami's insights was that "man is not traveling from error to truth, but climbing from truth to truth, from truth that is lower to truth that is higher." He was the precursor to the narrow, narcissistic spirituality that would explode in the 1960s and continue today. "Who can help you to the infinite?" Vivekananda asked. "Even the hand that comes to you through the darkness will have to be your own." Martin notes: "That [the swami] was religious in the pagan sense of that word was unimportant. [The appeal of the swami's philosophy] was that it harped on the dignity of man, the privileged power of reason; and it placed total trust only in human nature, so that if each person were free of all tinkering and tampering by organized religion, he could achieve his own happiness." It was the early version of the "I'm Okay" affirmation and happy hippie countercultures of the 1960s.

It was the acceptance of the extremes of modernism by certain radicals in the church, Martin maintains, that led to the ultimate collapse of the Jesuits. It began with a group of French Jesuits in the 1920s. They were the early version of the Berrigans. Calling themselves *La Pens ée* (thought), they met in private. By the 1940s reports were reaching the Vatican that there were members of the clergy who denied church teachings about original sin, the infallibility of the pope, and the divinity of Jesus. Pope Pius XII issued two encyclicals, *Mediatore Dei* and *Humani Generis*, that attacked modernism and reiterated the basic teachings of the church. Only years later was it revealed that the main target of the pope's words was *La Pensée*.

Perhaps the most prominent member of *La Pensée* was Pierre Teilhard de Chardin. Teilhard, as he called himself, was more of a New Age guru than a Jesuit priest. He was born in France in May 1881 and was ordained a priest at the age of thirty. Teilhard, who specialized in biology and paleontology, believed that the human race was evolving toward the "Omega Point" of history, when all individuals would be united as one. At that point Christ, the Omega Point, would appear. This idea of an inexorable evolution of mankind, complete with the bloodshed and revolutions that accompanied such action, fit nicely with the determinism of Marxism — naturally, Teilhard favored Communism. "Under the circumstances," he once said, "and in a capitalist world, how does one remain a Christian?" Teilhard claimed that "the Christian God on High and the Marxist god of progress are reconciled in Christ."

It's hardly surprising that Teilhard's writings were censored and even banned by Rome. What is surprising is that Teilhard became so well regarded among Jesuits. After all, these were the Pope's marines, the tough men who taught my father at Gonzaga. Teilhard advocated nothing short of overturning the core dogma and beloved rituals of the church. The very concept of God had to change, from Emmanuel, God among us, to the God of evolution who appears at the Omega Point. A priest was not necessary for conducting Mass and hearing a confession; after all, "savants are priests," and "[scientific] research is prayer, perhaps the highest form of prayer." In sexual matters, he was ahead of his time. He advocated eugenics, euthanasia, homosexuality, and *in vitro* fertilization. To him, humans have "the absolute right to try everything to the end — even in the matter of human biology."

Indeed, God almost seemed beside the point in Teilhard's cosmology. The true gods were human beings. People should embrace "the eternal human," because only by becoming more human can we become God. "I shall become the other only by being absolutely my own self. . . . I recognize that, in following the example of the incarnate God revealed to me by my Catholic faith, I can be saved only by becoming one with the universe."

This was a long way from the men who taught at Gonzaga. Teilhard was hugely influential, and by the 1960s his effect on the Jesuits was becoming increasingly obvious. In 1967 the Jesuits held a conference at the University of Santa Clara in California. Whether it was Vatican II or the contagion of radicalism brewing in the 1960s, the Jesuits made it increasingly clear that they had changed. The Jesuit magazine *America* supported the church's teachings on contraception until 1967, when it first published articles rejecting the teaching. The ground quickly began to shift in the late 1960s. The 1967 Santa Clara conference announced that the education of young Jesuits should emphasize "the needs of the present time in its fullness," including being up on contemporary American culture.

It's hardly surprising that Teilhard's writings were censored and even banned by Rome. What is surprising is that Teilhard became so well regarded among Jesuits.

Other recommendations of the conference would not be out of place at a New Age encounter group. The Jesuit community was to help each member "with his personal self-discovery, integration, and growth. Lack of openness with them will certainly preclude this possibility." In terms of prayer, the conference made a recommendation that directly contradicted the spiritual exercises of Ignatius Loyola. Prayer, the conference advised, should be directed at "the living Christ, now present in his people, rather than attempting to direct it to an imaginative recreation of the Jesus of 2000 years ago." In terms of education, there was virtually no emphasis placed on Catholic tradition. The conference all but demanded that the liturgy be radicalized. "Since liturgical adaptation and experimentation are of such pressing Apostolic importance, provincials should not content themselves with a permissive attitude in this matter, but [should] lead and, when necessary, exhort the superiors of our communities to similar leadership."

The real turning point for the Jesuits, however, came in 1974, during the thirty-second General Congregation, the gathering of Jesuits convened every few years. At the Congregation it was decided that the promotion of justice was central to being a Jesuit, not just one virtue among many. The Congregation also asserted that the failure to create a just world was simply due to a lack of will—a startlingly utopian statement for any Catholic to make. The Congregation also linked Christianity to oppression. "Part of the framework in which we have preached the gospel is now perceived as being inextricably linked to an unacceptable social order, and for that reason is being called into question." It's hardly surprising that Pope Paul VI told Pedro Arrupe y Gondra, the father general of the Jesuits, that he was afraid the Jesuits were neglecting the spiritual for the social and political. This Congregation also received a letter from Cardinal Jean Vinot stating that some of its decrees were "somewhat confusing" and could "give grounds for misinterpretation." He reminded the Jesuits not to forget the spiritual and supernatural foundations of the order.

The instruction didn't take, although in 1974 the society did dismiss one of its own, who had gone too far even by Jesuit standards. Joseph O'Rourke was a Jesuit who, upon his ordination in 1969, had refused the greeting of peace with Cardinal Cooke because of the latter's support for the Vietnam War. In 1974 O'Rourke disobeyed his Jesuit superiors when he traveled to Boston to baptize the baby of an employee of an abortion clinic — even after the Archdiocese of Boston had refused to authorize the baptism. Radical Jesuit Daniel Berrigan proclaimed that he would still consider O'Rourke a Jesuit; O'Rourke got support from other Jesuits and would go on to become a "court priest" to the pro-abortion movement.

By the 1970s dissent was as common among the Jesuits as black shirts. Jesuit magazines such as *America, Theological Studies*, England's *Month*, and *Etudes* in France published articles and essays that would have been at home in the radical secular press. In 1979 Walter Burghardt, editor of *Theological Studies*, claimed that he "choked" on the Vatican statement condemning contraception. In 1978 Jesuit theologian George Macowy claimed that the Eastern Orthodox

churches have "the saving feature of having avoided the heavy authority of a monarchical hierarchy under a pope." When in 1977
the Vatican issued a document explaining why women cannot be
priests, it was rejected by many Jesuits, including the entire faculty
of the Jesuit School of Theology in Berkeley. When in 1979 the
Vatican declared that the radical Swiss writer Hans Küng could no
longer be considered a Catholic theologian, a group of American
Jesuits signed a statement rejecting the Vatican decree and "affirming our recognition that Hans Küng is indeed a Roman Catholic
theologian."

It was also in 1979 that the pope came to visit America, including
Washington, D.C. The pope's motorcade would pass directly in front
of the *National Geographic* building, where my father worked. Dad
decided to make a day out of it and was actually more excited about
John Paul II's visit than Timothy Healy, the president of Georgetown
University, the oldest Catholic school in the United States. In the
December 8 issue of *America,* Healy announced that John Paul II
knew nothing about Catholic education. This would have been news
to my father, who considered John Paul II one of the great minds
of the twentieth century. While it would only be possible to catch
a glimpse of the pope as he passed in front of my father's building,
you would think that Dad was having a private audience with the
pontiff. Early on the morning of December 10 my father, myself, and
some friends went down to the *National Geographic* building. We had
breakfast in Dad's ninth floor office, and then the big moment came.
Down on the street, Dad holding my shoulders, I watched as the
pope, dressed in white, came riding through the canyon of buildings
on Seventeenth Street. "There he is!" Dad cried. It was a cold but
bright winter morning, and the sunlight reflected off the pope. He
looked like Gandalf, the good wizard in *The Lord of the Rings.*

At the time of the pope's visit, my father had steadily moved up
the masthead at *National Geographic,* going from writer to assistant
editor and then finally to associate editor. But his first love remained
writing.

By 1979 Dad had covered the world. He had written about, among
other places: Williamsburg, Israel, Borneo, Australia, Venice, Alaska,

Boston, and Florida. My favorite story of his was, and remains, the piece he did in April 1967 about his hometown, Washington, D.C. The piece focused on all the changes taking place in Washington in the 1960s. It was becoming an international city rather than a small town, as Dad discovered when he found out that his old neighborhood of Petworth, where he had lived until he was seven, had changed. Dad wrote:

> Like a good many natives of the nation's capital — buffeted by a civic change, jostled by national events, hounded by tourists, and elbowed by hordes of sophisticated newcomers — I am a perverse, provincial and melancholy man.
>
> I like few things better than a brooding afternoon at winter's end when the Congress is somnolent, the President is out of town, a raw mist shrouds the city's magnificent vistas, and a single sad bugle sings from Arlington's gray hill. Then might a native son pursue in peace his parochial grounds — to a silent Phillips Collection gallery to admire again that glass of ruby wine in Renoir's "Boating Party"; to an uncrowded Museum of Natural History to shudder before that Cheyenne necklace of human fingers; to the rare book room of the Library of Congress to reread the journal of Henry Spelman, slain by Indians along the Potomac in 1623; and finally to the lonely towpath of the Chesapeake and Ohio Canal where, in the last luminous light of a rifting sky, winter jasmine glows like a candle flame, setting early spring afire.
>
> No other kind of day will quite do, either, for that long journey into a man's past — to the old neighborhood of brick row houses where I spent the first seven years of my life. I had in mind a particular oak I longed to see....
>
> I do believe my heart skipped a full beat when I turned the final corner. The old oak was not there. My first home was not there. The entire block where once had lived the McCarthys, the Rices, the Judges, the Walkers, the Petrones was not there anymore. In its place was a rubble-strewn lot where a damp wind casually folded the pages of a month-old newspaper.

Forlorn, I stumbled through the pulverized brick until I found a friend, a battered lamppost still standing. In those bygone years, it had served as third base in our stickball games. As I leaned against it, remembering evenings thick with fireflies when we gathered there to play "kick the can," a small boy sauntered by on his way home from [my old school] St. Gabriel's. . . . I summoned him.

"Why did they knock these houses down?"

He considered for a moment. "I expect they're knocking the whole town down,"

"Nobody asked me about it," I said.

He shouldered his book pack, mumbled to himself, and went on his way.

They were also knocking down the Catholic Church Dad had known, although he wasn't aware of it. Like so many members of his generation, he trusted the church. He felt comfortable that in sending me to Georgetown Prep I would get the same education he had gotten at Gonzaga. In one way he was right. Prep is a school steeped in history, family, friendship, and tradition. Many of the hundred boys in my class had gone to parochial school together. Our parents had gone to Gonzaga, Georgetown Visitation, and the other Catholic schools in the area. Many of our older brothers had also gone to Prep. I'll never forget when I was in the eighth grade and had an interview as part of my application. I sat down with my parents in front of a teacher I had never met before. "You're a little taller than your brothers," he said after shaking my hand. "But I bet you're not as good an actor as your brother."

This kind of atmosphere led to a sense of being part of a group that knew you even better than you knew yourself. There was also the advantage of Prep being an all-boys school. At a critical time in our lives we were allowed to study, make friends, and get to know girls as friends due, paradoxically, to the fact that we were not distracted by girls. At age fifteen it was hard to think of anything else. And had there been girls on campus, Prep would not have been the place it was.

The school was the brainchild of John Carroll, the first bishop of Baltimore. In the 1780s Carroll, who had been born into one of Maryland's wealthiest families, set about to create a school for young men that would accomplish two goals: to give the boys a liberal (in the classical sense) education that would let them become leaders in social, economic, and cultural areas of the New World; to create a "seed-ground of vocations" by teaching the students the Catholic faith. In fact, to Carroll the second goal was more important than the first. "The Jesuits of Georgetown regarded the Christian formation of students as their primary mission," writes the author of *Academy on the Potowmack: Georgetown Preparatory School 1789–1927*. "Knowledge and skills, although important, were approached as means to an end: the knowledge and love of God. Jesuit teachers sought to mold Georgetown students during their formative years into Christian citizens who would act as leaven in the world."

Both points of Carroll's plan were virtually nonexistent by the time I arrived at Prep in 1979. The school was divided between the old Jesuit tradition and the new. The courses I took my first year were taught by men, both Jesuit and not, who had been at the school for decades, so the curriculum was similar to what my father had taken at Gonzaga: Latin, Shakespeare, speech class, debate. The one glaring omission was religion — there simply was none. Our catechism freshman year consisted of a talk by an old priest whose claim to fame was that he had been a technical advisor to the film *The Exorcist*. His talk was spurred by several members of the senior class who had gotten their girlfriends pregnant. The priest sat on the edge of the teacher's desk in the front of the room and told us about the poor guys. His advice was that if we ever got into similar trouble we should come talk to him. There was no talk of chastity, no discussion of the brilliant work of John Paul II, who had written so remarkably on love and responsibility. No. If our hormones got the best of us, we were to have a therapy session.

By the time I made it to Prep, a lot of the tough guys like Gonzaga's Father Herlihy had been replaced by hippies and leftists — although a few traces of the old order remained. I'll never forget two in particular. I'll call them Father Boxer and Father Moon. Father

Boxer had once been a boxer, and the three things he loved most in the world were Jesus, America, and discipline. My freshman year, 1979, saw the hostage crisis in Iran, and one afternoon the clock in Father Boxer's algebra class kept making clacking noises. Finally Father Boxer slammed his hand on the desk. "Good God!" he bellowed. "That noise is like what they would do to me in a goddam Iranian cell!"

Our catechism freshman year consisted of a talk by an old priest whose claim to fame was that he had been a technical advisor to the film The Exorcist.

The other Jesuit, Father Moon, was a stocky German who could not have been more than five feet five inches tall. One afternoon on the bus ride home a bunch of us started mooning the cars behind us. Our driver was not a Jesuit, just some guy the school had hired. But he spilled the beans the next day. That afternoon, after we had all taken our seats on the bus as usual, Father Moon climbed the stairs and stood to face us. "*If I hear one report,*" he hissed, the bus falling silent in a millisecond, "of a *single one* of you *little bastards* dropping your pants and showing your *asses* to the world, I'm going to make sure that your asses get so red in JUG [Justice Under God, our form of detention] that you won't be able to sit down in this *goddam* bus for the next four *f***ing* years."

Nobody breathed.

The most famous teacher at Prep was Mr. James. He was four feet eleven inches tall, weighed about a hundred pounds, and was as bald as Don Rickles. From the dawn of time Mr. James had taught English, Latin, and speech classes at Prep. He taught our older brothers who had gone to Prep, as well as our uncles, fathers, and ever grandfathers.

Mr. James had been old as long as anyone could remember, but he had the vivaciousness of a teenager. He had a sandpaper voice, and when he was coming down the hall he sounded like the world's

most upbeat drill sergeant. "How-do, brother!" was his favorite greeting, and he had a series of catch phrases that he used to motivate
us. When someone didn't know an answer, he would cry, "Come
outta the fog, brother!" If a student was well prepared and could rifle
through his Latin verbs, he would urge him on — "Go, man, go!" He
drove a gigantic old Cadillac, and needed three phone books on the
seat so he could see over the steering wheel.

Mr. James was an old school Catholic teacher. He stuck to Shakespeare and memorization of Latin words while other teachers were
pushing to teach *The Catcher in the Rye.* Mr. James would often go
off on a tangent about the proper way for "a civilized person" to be-
have, whether it was holding a chair while a lady sat down or steering
clear of guys who cussed or wrote graffiti. His speech class was one
of the remnants of my dad's Catholic education, when the ability to
stand and articulate a position was considered a virtue and shyness
something to overcome, not medicate. For speech class he would
videotape us delivering our speeches and then critique the tape in
front of the entire class. I was so nervous delivering my speech —
I think it was a recitation of something from Shakespeare — that I
kept swaying back and forth. From his tiny desk in the front corner of
the room, Mr. James roasted me: "Who's got the next dance, Judge?
You're jumpin' around like a monkey on a stick!"

None of this was ever said with cruelty — indeed, quite the opposite. Mr. James loved students as much as any teacher I've ever had.
To be sure, he didn't put up with any foolishness in his classroom, but
he was eager to be friends with his charges. Once during the middle
of an exam a student near the front farted loudly. He was one of
the best students, and it had been a genuine accident. He started
stammering and sweating and apologizing, expecting to be sent to
the dean. Mr. James just smiled and waved it off. "Don't worry about
it, Smyth," he growled. "It happens in the best of families." When
he caught someone imitating him, he didn't punish the student; he
critiqued the imitation and told him to work harder on it. Mr. James
had given me a JUG detention a couple times for talking in class.
Then one afternoon he asked me to stay after the bell rang. I though
I was about to get a tongue lashing. Instead, he handed me a paper I

had written on *Romeo and Juliet*. He had given me an A. "Best paper in the class, Judgie," he said. "So stop acting like you're not serious and you can't do it. I know you can do it, and you know you can do it."

These teachers were the last traces of Catholicism at the school. One night I got a call from a friend of mine from English class. "Have you read the assigned book for this week?" he said. I hadn't. It was something called *The Catcher in the Rye*. I knew nothing about it, but I was sure it would be dull. "Start it right now!" my friend cried. "It's incredible! This guy farts in church! It's unreal!"

The Catcher in the Rye is indeed a wonderful book, and I have no criticism of its inclusion in any high school curriculum. What I now find disturbing is that the book was not balanced by a curriculum that included great Catholic books — *The Man Who Was Thursday* by Chesterton, the space trilogy by C. S. Lewis, *Brideshead Revisited* by Evelyn Waugh. From *The Catcher in the Rye* we went not to Tolkien's *The Lord of the Rings* but to *The Lord of the Flies*, another book about juvenile delinquency.

Incredibly, all this was happening in the wake of a powerful apostolic exhortation on catechesis issued by the pope in 1979. *Catechesi Tradendae* (Catechesis in Our Time) was a bracing attempt to reemphasize the central purpose of any kind of Catholic teaching. Part 1 of section 1 spelled it out in big bold letters: "We Have But One Teacher, Jesus Christ." "The primary and essential object of catechesis," the pope wrote, "is, to use an expression dear to St. Paul and also to contemporary theology, 'The mystery of Christ.' Catechizing is, in a way, to lead a person to study this mystery in all its dimensions: 'to make all men see what is the plan of the mystery...comprehend with all the saints what is the breadth and length and height and depth...know the love of Christ which surpasses knowledge....'"

The pope then outlined how this was to be done. As mentioned, Christ was the center of all catechesis. Catechism must be "systematic, not improvised but programmed to reach a precise goal." It must "deal with essentials." Without shutting out the importance of personal experience, the focus must remain on Christ.

Authentic catechesis is always an orderly and systematic ini-
tiation into the revelation that God has given of Himself to
humanity in Christ Jesus, a revelation stored in the depths of
the Church's memory and in Sacred Scripture, and constantly
communicated from one generation to the next by a living, active *traditio*. This revelation is not, however, isolated from life
or artificially juxtaposed to it. It is concerned with the ultimate
meaning of life and it illuminates the whole of life with the light
of the Gospel, to inspire it or to question it.

The pope acknowledged the mistakes that had been made and
emphasized the importance of children and young people in the process of catechesis. "In certain places," he wrote, "the desire to find
the best forms of expression or to keep up with fashions in pedagogi-
cal methods has often enough resulted in certain catechetical works
which bewilder the young and even adults, either by deliberately or
unconsciously omitting elements essential to the Church's faith, or
by attributing excessive importance to certain themes at the expense
of others, or, chiefly, by a rather horizontalist overall view out of
keeping with the teaching of the Church's magisterium." The pope
even defended memorization: "the blossoms . . . of faith and piety do
not grow in the desert places of a memory-less catechesis."

None of this trickled down to Prep — but sex and drugs did. Coming of age after the 1960s, we were still caught in the riptide of the
drug culture. In his book *The Decline and Fall of Radical Catholicism*, James Hitchcock warned of the problem of drift: "Few Catholic
radicals appear to have any principles, or any basic strategy, for deal-
ing with the problem of drift — the process by which beliefs, ways
of living, and values change not through any reasoned argument or
profound life experience but simply because the culture itself changes
and the individual has no resources for resisting the tide, indeed has
come to believe that such resistance is futile and unnecessary." Hitchcock claimed that drift would be especially lethal for the upcoming
generation — "The force of the culture, and especially the youth culture, will be virtually irresistible in the lives of many individuals who
are not likely to be happier, freer, or more creative as a result."

Thanks to my father, however, I could not avoid Christ. After my first year at Prep *National Geographic* published a story on the Shroud of Turin, the garment that many claim is the burial cloth of Christ. One night I woke up at about 3 a.m., thirsty for a glass of water. I padded downstairs. Dad had left the light on in his study when he had gone to bed. I noticed some photographs laid out on his desk and crept in to investigate. They were photos that had been used in the story about the shroud. One of them has become iconic. It is the black-and-white negative of the face on the shroud — possibly the face of Jesus.

I sat down, riveted by the photograph. I knew that as a Christian I had to go to Mass, be nice to people, and not have sex too much before marriage. But one thing had been missing from my Catholic education: Jesus Christ. But there was now a new pope, one who would dedicate himself to the rediscovery of the ever ancient, ever new truth of Christ, the eternal revolution.

I looked at the photograph for a few minutes, then went back to bed, and by the next day forgot all about it. As the 1980s began, so did the party at Prep.

— Chapter Five —

Rock and Roll

In Frank Sheed's 1974 classic *The Church and I*, the reader gets a bracing example of what was once required to be a knowledgeable Catholic. Sheed, born in 1897, was one of the great Catholic apologists — that is to say, promoters — of the twentieth century. He ran the publishing house Sheed & Ward, once one of the finest Catholic houses in the world.

What's remarkable about *The Church and I* is Sheed's description of how he became such a skilled spokesman for his faith. Sheed grew up in Australia as a kind of rote Catholic, someone who loves the church but doesn't quite know why. "I loved the Church then as I always have," he wrote. "But I did not then know what the Church *is*."

This changed in the early 1920s when Sheed, then in his twenties, traveled to England. There he went to a concert sponsored by the Catholic Evidence Guild. Members of the Guild would hold rallies and concerts or simply stand on a soapbox in the park and defend their faith. On his first exposure, Sheed was appalled — not at the speakers but at his own ignorance. After going back several times to listen, he joined the Guild and became a speaker.

Sheed's accounts of his detractors make even the most virulent anti-Christian — or just anti-religious — bigot of today seem like St. Francis in comparison. In the pre–sensitivity-training 1920s, audiences addressed by the Guild were often made up of the most malevolent foes, many having been sent specifically to heckle the speakers. Unlike today, when hecklers are quickly escorted from debates, Sheed and his colleagues had different rules: they spoke for fifteen minutes and then for forty-five minutes answered all questions, no matter how hostile. Indeed, part of the private training was being mock-heckled by two priests before graduating to speaking in public.

Sheed faced it all — intellectual debunkers, comic pranksters, and outright lunatics. One night Sheed was having trouble speaking because of a cough. "Excuse me, sir," a heckler said. "I think there's something wrong with your throat. If I were you, I'd get it cut." ("After forty years I have not been able to come up with a snappy return," Sheed writes.) People at the foot of the platform untied his shoelaces and tied them to the podium. The audience drilled the speaker with questions and arguments about every conceivable facet of Catholic dogma — the pope, the Immaculate Conception, infallibility, the Holy Spirit. If a speaker didn't know the answer, he had to go home, find the answer, and come back the next week and report it to the crowd. After one lecture a man followed Sheed back to the train station muttering, "Next week I'll bring my son to thrash you. I'd do it myself if I wasn't a Christian." Sheed reports only one time when a speaker heckled back. A woman in the crowd accused the local priest of "sending young men from the confessional to make love to me." "I didn't know they gave out such severe penances nowadays," the speaker replied. "We didn't find it in our hearts to censure him," writes Sheed.

Through this theological boot camp Sheed learned his faith with a depth that was foreign to most Catholics — even in the days of the *Baltimore Catechism* and strict memorization of the faith. His distinction between types of learning is instructive: "My university years in arts and law gave me one kind of formation. The writers I met in over forty years' publishing gave me another. But the crowds forced a general intellectual and specifically theological development not to be had elsewhere. One had to examine every doctrine — not only to answer the questioners but to relate Christ's revelation to their appallingly various natures, in order that they might discover unrealized needs in themselves and find those needs met in Christ. Very early we learned that we could not meet their depths in our shallows."

Sheed, no liberal, goes so far as to claim that the radical explosion that took place in the church after Vatican II was precipitated, at least in part, by the crackdown against modernism initiated by Pope Pius X in 1907. Many modernist claims, notes Sheed, were rejected out of hand but not responded to. As a result, both sides hardened their positions without being forced to debate.

Sheed also taps into something profound with his observation that his opponents contained depths. Growing up Catholic, as a child I had no trouble believing the dogma of the church. When I reached adolescence I began to lose my faith. I now realize that this was the result of not having to make a transition, such as Sheed had, from passively to actively accepting the teachings of the church. Like every other Catholic — indeed like every other human — I contained the depths to appreciate and love God and all his wonders. Those depths were not only not filled by Catholic teachers; they were often misunderstood as being sins.

Looking back, I remember one particular time in my life when I took a step away from my faith — or rather, what I conceived to be a step away from my faith. In fact, in many ways I was stepping deeper into the mystery of Christ. There was plenty of sin mixed in as well, yet it wasn't, as I often thought of it, pure debauchery.

Every summer the Catholic kids would go to the Eastern Shore of Maryland for a week in June, before the public schools would let out for the summer. In 1980, my sophomore year at Georgetown Prep, a group of us got a place in Ocean City, Maryland. We also managed to hoodwink our parents — our chaperone could not have been more than thirty. This man — I'll call him Steve — was a teacher at a well-known all-boys grammar school in Maryland. That much we told our parents, who happily signed off on the trip. What we didn't mention was that Steve let us know two things on the very first day: he would buy us as much beer as we could drink (providing we were paying), and we were not allowed to drive anywhere if we had been drinking.

There was nothing sinister or malevolent about Steve — indeed, quite the opposite. He was a sweet, jovial man who never lost his temper. It's also important to note that in 1980 the legal drinking age in Maryland was eighteen. Many of us had started sneaking beers at parties from the time we were freshmen. My best friend had been in the school production of 1776 when we were freshmen, and he'd come home tipsy from a couple of cast parties. His parents knew that Jesuits had been at the parties and didn't get overly worried about it. We were all members of the Prep family.

At beach week with Steve, all bets were off. The party started already on the trip down. I got a ride with my best friend, Tommy, and his older sister, who drove the three hours down to Ocean City. She also bought a case of beer, which Tommy and I started to drink. I guzzled about five beers, and the next thing I knew it was two hours later and I was waking up. We were still in the car and on the way to the beach, but it was two hours later. I needed to relieve myself so badly I wasn't sure I could wait until Tommy's sister pulled the car off to the side of the road. When she did, Tommy (who had also passed out) and I tumbled out. There was a patch of woods about fifty yards off the busy highway, but my leg had fallen asleep. I could barely stand up — and it didn't help that I was still drunk. I still remember the cars honking as they drove past, watching me trying to go to the bathroom and shake my leg awake at the same time.

For the next seven days a new world came to life. Without parents, without even a serious chaperone, we were allowed to enter into a different reality. We ate whatever and whenever we wanted, got drunk at night and in the middle of the day, and chased girls without fear of a curfew or punishment. Several Catholic girls' schools also had groups down — on one side of our place was a group from Georgetown Visitation, on the other a group from the School of the Holy Child in Maryland. Unlike us, however, in most cases the girls were accompanied by serious chaperones or even parents.

I have been careful not to describe the trip as my first step into debauchery or as the initial phase of a flight from God. Certainly there was plenty of sinning going on. But the main sensation of the experience was the discovery of new modes of love. The highest, of course, was the absolute fecundity of God's love for his creatures, as expressed in the miracle of the world itself. The great theologian Jean Daniélou has observed that "creation is the first revelation." At the beach the splendor and self-giving force of this creation was evident. Our every day revolved around this splendor. In the morning we would bring our blankets down to the beach to lie in the sun — which, as Chesterton noted, dances in the sky. We would spend hours in the surf, surrendering ourselves to the embrace of the waves until we were so stupefied with fatigue that we trudged like old men back to our blankets. At exactly the same time every day, two o'clock — it was never planned, it just seemed to happen that way — we climbed to the second-story balcony of the house to play drinking games for a couple of hours, a perverse Liturgy of the Hours. Then it was a nap, dinner — most likely, fast food — and a shower and a shave to get ready for that night's party. Through it all the laughter never stopped.

What is so sad about this is that we considered this new joy an escape from God rather than an entrance into God's self-giving mystery. The deep sensuality occasioned by a place like the beach — the brief, rapturous loss of breath when one is smothered by a wave; the feel of sand under the toes; the unquenchable grandeur of the plain of the ocean illuminated by the moonlight — all herald the closeness of the Maker. This was evident to Ignatius Loyola, about whom we had read nothing at Georgetown Prep. Loyola celebrated and encouraged the practice of "seeing God in all things" — even in the nautical world.

The wonderful Jesuit theologian Jacques Servais explored this in an essay published in the Catholic journal *Communio*. St. Ignatius encouraged Christians to "seek our Lord in all things, detaching themselves as far as possible from the love of all creatures in order to place their love in the Creator of these creatures, loving Him in all things, and all things in Him, in conformity to His very holy and divine will." What this means, according to Servais, is not the rejection of the world, but the conversion of the love of earthly things — "vain honor," as Servais calls them — to a love of things as an expression of the love of Christ. Ignatius preached that the Christian journey begins when a person is "wrested from the perilous sea of the world . . . which stirs the wind of the desire for wealth, honors, and pleasures." But it doesn't end there. After his conversion the

Christian is sent back into the world to love God in all things, certain, according to Ignatius, that he will find God "in all things, even the earthly and lowly things, if [he] loves them all for the Lord our God and to the extent to which they work towards His greater glory and service." Although only human beings are created in the image of God, other creatures are "vestiges" of God. "Everything has been created by Him and for Him, and He Himself is above all things; all things have their being in Him," as Servais so beautifully explains, referring to Corinthians.

To the eyes of faith, far from being a thing that God would simply have abandoned after having created it, the world appears as a reality that he continues to sustain in existence, a reality through which he desires to give himself "as much as he is able according to His divine plan." The universe, in its apparently closed and prideful immanance has sprung from top to bottom from the fullness of God. That which seems to be pure absence and emptiness is the expression of a delicate, discrete, and gentle proximity. Indeed, God allows the created reality to be itself: He gives it totally, without reserve, without holding back, to itself, and in a certain way withdraws himself behind the gift that he offers, so that man might find there the space in which his freedom is able to come into its own.

That space — the world — is sacred, and even as a young teenager I could see the divine superiority of a place like the beach to some of the bland and ugly suburbs back home. I've heard conservatives, even conservative Catholics, fulsomely make the argument that eyesores such as highways and Wal-Marts are not only good for America, but even holy. It is utilitarianism as the sacred: Wal-Mart creates a lot of jobs. It sells a lot of stuff. It is, *ipso facto,* good. In a cover story in the *National Review* Jay Norlinger itemizes the criticisms — that Wal-Mart is a bad employer, "crassly American," and even "vulgar" — then offers a robust defense: "Wal-Mart is gloriously, unabashedly, star-spangledly American. I hope it's not too McCarthyite to suggest that those who dislike Wal-Mart are those who may not be so crazy about America *tout court.*"

Here is a conservative who can admonish liberals for their lack of sense, courage, loyalty, and virtue, yet who seems incapable of seeing how an architectural eyesore is bad for the soul — and, conversely, how a beautiful building is good for the soul. Such thinkers ignore the sacredness of beauty in deference to the virtue of capitalism, even if that virtue is ugly. To conservatives, the beautiful is tied in with the virtues of Middle America — humility, gratitude, discount prices. And they are right that these things — or at least the first two — are beautiful. But also important to the soul is artistic and natural beauty. The great twentieth-century theologian and Nazi-fighter Dietrich von Hildebrand explored this in an essay, "Beauty in the Light of the Redemption." In it he rejected the purely utilitarian, Wal-Mart view of beauty:

> An estimate of all things from the viewpoint of their practical and absolute necessity ... is to be found neither in God's creation nor in the revelation of Christ. In these, on the contrary, the principle of superabundance rules. Is God not lavish in His creation? Is beauty in nature not the clearest proof of this divine profusion, since it is in no way practically indispensable in the economy of nature? ... Is it not the pure emanation of the infinite love of God and in no way necessary? The first miracle of Christ at the wedding feast of Cana reveals to us in a glorious manner the superabundance of divine love, which shows no restriction to that which is necessary. The wine was not at all indispensable to the wedding feast. Does not the fact that the content of the miracle has reference only to heightening the resplendence of the feast imply a radical renunciation of all forms of utilitarianism? The fact that beauty of form is not indispensable does not affect its value or its seriousness.

One central irony in all this is that conservatives consider themselves hard-nosed realists who "see the world as it really is." But the value and seriousness of beauty is not that it is a sensual and fantastic escape from reality. To von Hildebrand, audible and visible things — some of his favorites are Tuscan villas, the frescoes of Masaccio in the Carmine, Mozart's *The Marriage of Figaro,* and Beethoven's Ninth Symphony —

are not an escape from but a plunge into reality. As von Hildebrand says, these things "do more than point to the good; they herald God." At the time I made no connection that the beach could herald Christ. Of course, in the eyes of young post-1960s Catholic kids Christ was limited — he was our Savior who had died on the cross two thousand years ago. What was more appealing than Christ was the recurring charge we got from the world directly around us. We were never told what Ignatius had said: "consider how God labors and works for me in all created things." Further, we were not aware that it is not possible to limit Christ — indeed, this was not possible even for those who met him face to face. The great twentieth-century Christian mystic Adrienne von Speyr once noted that to the crowds who meet Jesus in the Bible, the meeting is not an end but a simple point of departure. "They seek Him like those who have encountered Him one day, those who one day were touched by His grace. . . . They seek the Lord even though they are in His presence and have found Him." Von Speyr explains that "one side of [Christ's] being always allows itself only to be ever again sought, even when it had already been found. . . . The one who recognizes the Lord has to seek Him as ever-greater."

To my generation, Christ had become ever smaller; indeed, he had been stripped of his divinity. In the book *We Follow Jesus*, a third-grade reader used in Catholic schools in the early 1970s, a passage from the Bible, Luke 10:38–42, is given as follows:

Martha and Mary were close friends of Jesus. Mary was talking to Jesus. Martha came to Jesus She was worried about cooking the dinner. "Jesus, get Mary to help me," said Martha. But Jesus said: "Now, Martha, do not worry too much about dinner; just do the best you can."

This is how the passage actually reads in the Bible:

And a woman named Martha received him into her house. And she had a sister called Mary, who sat at the Lord's feet and listened to his teaching. But Martha was distracted with much serving; and she went to him and said, "Lord, do you not care that my sister has left me to serve alone? Tell her then to help me." But the Lord answered her, "Martha, Martha, you are anxious and troubled about many things; one thing is needful. Mary has chosen the good portion, which shall not be taken away from her."

In the first example, the point of the story is entirely lost. Jesus is reduced from the Son of God to a modern sensitive man who tells Martha she worries too much and should just do the best she can. As von Hildebrand points out in *The Charitable Anathema*, the Word and Worship series, of which *We Follow Jesus* was a part, also omits references to sanctification, eternal life, God's judgment, beatitude, even hell. One of the books placed Christ on a list of other famous men: "George Washington is famous because he was a great general. Daniel Boone is famous because he was a great Indian scout. Babe Ruth is famous as a great baseball player. Many men are famous for many different reasons. Jesus Christ, however, is famous because he loved people so much."

This was the vague, wispy Christ whom we were introduced to as children. We learned to see him in church but nowhere else — not in the beach, in our friends, or in the face of a beautiful girl. But like everyone else, we knew instinctively that these things were images and vestiges of God. We were never taught the value of what C. S. Lewis called need-love, which is a particularly acute form of love found in teenagers. In his book *The Four Loves*, Lewis writes that he once believed there are two kinds of love — give-love, which is the divine love God gives to us, and need-love, which stems from human need and our helpless nature. Lewis had regarded the first love as good and the second bad. But then he realized that man's love, from the very nature of the case, is need-love. This is the way we are made, to have potent desires for sensual and aesthetic connection with things in the world as vestiges of God. Even our lower forms of need-love, like the appreciation of great art, point toward an ultimate beauty and come to us through our senses. Thus to gift-love and need-love is added the additional category of appreciative love. Appreciative love can stand back from a person or thing and wonder at its beauty and be glad for its existence. That stepping back, and that gladness, bespeaks what Lewis calls a "disinterestedness": "It is the feeling which would make a man unwilling to deface a great picture even if he were the last man left alive and himself about to die." Thus even our "lowest" need-loves can remind us of God. The point is to be mindful of loving gifts that come from God and not to mistake these things for God himself. As Lewis puts it, we are not to mistake, "like for same." "We may give our human loves the unconditional allegiance which we owe only to God," Lewis writes. "Then they become gods; then they become demons. Then they will destroy us, and also destroy themselves."

> We learned to see Christ in church but nowhere else — not in the beach, in our friends, or in the face of a beautiful girl.

From that first beach week through the next ten years, this is basically what happened to me. My Catholic schooling simply did not educate me that joy, friendship, and the powerful attraction to the opposite sex were natural and healthy reactions to the manifestations of the Creator. These things were the best things in life, and Christ had been minimized to the point where I could not see him in the world. When this happens the things that God created offer diminishing returns. When there is no longer a hierarchy of loves with God at the top, those lesser loves become gods who cannot satisfy.

We simply lacked the proper language, which is spiritual language, to describe the ardor of being young and alive in the world that God has made sacred. We didn't consider our friendships to be expressions of Christian virtue. We knew we lusted after girls, but we had no idea that the pope had written brilliantly on the role of human sexuality in God's plan. At our parties that were full of laughter that went all night, at our homecoming dances, or during the magic of Christmas Eve, we had little idea that the things we were experiencing had any interpretation in the Catholic Church. It would be years after I graduated from Prep and began to read some of the great Catholic thinkers who had never been taught in my Catholic schools that I understood the sense of joy and wonder I often experienced in high school and after.

I had no idea there was something sacred in the party that began down at the beach. Josef Pieper writes in his book *In Tune with the World: A Theory of Festivity*: "Underlying all festive joy kindled by a specific circumstance," he writes, "there was to be an absolute universal affirmation extending to the world as a whole, to the reality of things and the existence of man himself." The ultimate foundation of the festive spirit, Pieper observes, is the idea that "everything that is, is good, and it is good·to exist." Pieper then does what few of the Jesuits of the 1980s would do. He brings God into the picture.

> Incidentally, there is a kind of confirmation of this from the other shore, as it were. Whenever we happen to feel heartfelt assent, to find that something specific is good, wonderful, glorious, rapturous — a drink of fresh water, the precise functioning of a tool, the colors of a landscape, the charm of a loving gesture, a poem — our praise always reaches beyond the given object, if matters take their natural course. Our tribute always contains at least a smattering of affirmation of the world, as a whole.

Pieper then notes how the "quality of this assent" was present in the Christian martyrs. "What distinguished the Christian martyr is that he never utters a word against God's creation." That is why the martyr can retain joy, even festivity, even while under "brutal assault." Conversely, "festivity is impossible to the nay-sayer. The more money he has, and above all the more leisure, the more desperate is this impossibility to him."

As for religion, ours was rock and roll. We were surrounded by pop music virtually all of the time. We had been raised not only by our parents but by those who had greater influence on us — our older brothers and sisters who had come of age in the 1960s and 1970s. For them and for us, the music was our faith. We knew the lives and worlds of Mick Jagger, Bob Dylan, and Bruce Springsteen the way medieval scholars knew the lives of the saints. Ridiculously, we thought we were somehow rebellious in embracing rock rather than our faith.

In the essay "Life in the Stone Age," critic Louis Menand underscores the point that the rock and roll "counterculture" is not a counterculture at all, but rather a mainstream culture, in fact a religious sect with its own orthodoxy — an orthodoxy far more restrictive and intolerant than the conservative and religious orthodoxies against which rock-and-rollers are always waging social battles. I've brought this point up myself in articles, a book, and on the radio. (On NPR, the host seemed baffled at my observation that rock culture has rules — right down to the dress code — that are every bit as strict as a Carmelite order.) Menand makes the point with considerable skill:

> The general idea [of the 1960s counterculture] was the rejection of the norms of adult middle-class life; but the rejection was made in a profoundly middle-class spirit. Middle-class Americans are a driven, pampered, puritanical, self-indulgent group of people. Before the sixties, these contradictions were rationalized by the principle of deferred gratification: you exercised self-discipline in order to gain entrance to a profession. You showed deference to those above you on the career ladder, and material rewards followed and could be enjoyed more or less promiscuously. To many people, the counterculture alternative looked like simple hedonism: sex, drugs, and rock 'n' roll (with some instant social justice on the side). But the counterculture wasn't hedonistic; it was puritanical. It was, for that matter, virtually Hebraic: the parents were worshipping false gods, and the students who tore up (or dropped out of) the university in an apparent frenzy of self-destruction — for wasn't the university their gateway to the good life? — were, in effect, smashing the golden calf.

In place of the calf, the 1960s generation erected "the new god of authenticity." This god "demanded an existence of programmatic hostility to the ordinary modes of middle-class life, and even to the ordinary modes of consciousness — to whatever was mediated, accommodationist, materialistic, and, even trivially, false." Menand notes that "there are two places in American society where this strain of Puritanism persists" — the academy, and pop music criticism.

The loss of Christianity in favor of the rock-and-roll god of authenticity happened to countless Catholic kids. One of the best known was Ann Powers, a gifted writer who became the rock-and-roll music critic for the *New York Times*. Powers and I are of the same generation, and her book *Weird Like Us: My Bohemian America* (2000) reflects what my attitudes were as a young person, and shows how so many Catholic kids of her and my generation don't know their faith.

Powers was raised Catholic and went to Catholic school, but her education was no better than mine. Instead, she gravitated to the rock-and-roll culture: "Without that music, so mysterious in its multiple languages of the boutique, the dancehall, and the alleyway, and yet so easily explored via radio and record store, I might never have learned to make myself into a person. Forever, I would have remained the overweight outcast who published her poems in the Our Lady of Fatima grade-school newspaper but didn't have any friends."

Like so many of us, Powers believed that the natural joy and intoxication one feels upon hearing a great song has its deepest meaning as a call for radical social change. Powers moved to San Francisco and became a journalist. She experimented with drugs, hung out in Bohemian dives, and advocated left-wing political causes. The last of these came to constitute the sum total of Powers's life, the central and animating force of her personality. The personal was the political, and politics was her religion. At her wedding, a pagan ceremony, it seemed more important to her to reject traditional forms of marriage than to affirm something timeless about the complementary and stereotypical roles of men and women. She defends pornography, drug-taking, and other vices in the name of freedom, not realizing that they are actually forms of bondage.

Yet the most arresting part of Powers's book is the ending. She describes how many of her Bohemian dreams, such as "a world without conflict, friends who don't disappoint or become drug addicts," led to disillusionment, but this sharp and talented writer refuses to admit that such experiences might lead to a repudiation of her narrow, intolerant ideology and a fresh, and ancient, wisdom about the true meaning of human freedom. Powers gets a job at the *New York Times*, but quits to work for the radical weekly the *Village Voice*. She soon discovers that the *Voice* is a "dysfunctional family" where "deep attachment to your work is often expected to substitute for reasonable pay, hours, public recognition, and benefits." Rather than concluding that no matter how politically pure any organization claims to be, human nature is tainted with sin and therefore doesn't change. Powers blames the problems at the *Voice* on "the pressures of the free market."

Powers also refuses to acknowledge human nature in her discussion of love and marriage. She notes that several of her friends got married and had children, but refuses to acknowledge that this may have changed them at all. One couple who found themselves accused of selling out when they announced their nuptials had this strange reaction: "The pair blushes, mumbling about health insurance, the bride insisting that she won't be wearing white." Another friend starts directing a movie nine months after giving birth. Most poignant is the case of Cassandra and Dennis. The two Bohemians got married in an unconventional ceremony and were living a life of "bliss" when Dennis was injured at work, an accident that made it difficult for him to get around. Then they had a child. To Dennis, "coping with all these things makes it really interesting. The way you go about your life together becomes a whole different thing." Sounds like the two rebels grew up. Yet Powers gets only one lesson: "If Dennis and Cassandra's bond had really been formed along traditional gender lines, this crisis would have sunk them." Contrary to the sentiments expressed by her subjects, Powers insists that one never has to change or grow up.

What is frustrating about this is that Powers's view is considered the option of freedom and joy, when in fact it is a dead end. *Weird Like Us* opens with a quote from the rock singer Juliana Hatfield: "Become what you are." In the context of Powers's arguments, this seems to mean: become what you are when you are a fifteen-year-old. Age, injury, the arrival of children — all these things should be a spur to indulge in the narcissism and protests that were part of life as a college student. Powers then wants Bohemians to bring this attitude to the larger culture. Drug use, premarital sex, homosexuality, prostitution, and pornography are "meaningless if you think only in terms of an impossible revolution, but crucial to the incremental process through which society actually changes." Apparently, becoming what we are means changing everybody else.

A few years after I returned to the church, I came across the same phrase — "become what you are" — but in a far different context. It appears as the heading of a section in the book *The Conjugal Act as a Personal Act,* by Donald P. Asci, a professor of theology at the Franciscan University of Steubenville. The book deals with the theology of sex, offering a perspective that is much more real and human than Powers's. Citing the work of John Paul II, Asci explains that the conjugal act "reveals what it means to be a person." During that act "the person is revealed to be self-gift in love." It is in making himself a gift that "man becomes who God wills him to be and, thus, lives out this vocation."

In other words, to truly become what you are means to lose yourself to another in love. In essence, it means the exact opposite of what Powers claims. Yet perhaps the greatest irony of all is that when one listens to pop songs, it soon becomes clear that the best of them reinforce rather than challenge orthodox Catholicism. I'll never forget the ecstasy of dancing to those songs at beach week, or the time, a few years after I graduated from high school, when I heard the song "Under the Milky Way" by the aptly named Australian group the Church. It was 1987, and I was in college and working in a record store in Washington, D.C. After work one night I went to a nearby bar. I ordered a beer, and suddenly "Under the Milky Way" came over the stereo. I felt that magical tremor that occurs when one hears not a good pop song or even a great one, but an immortal one. I was transported into another world. I entered the mystique. I was in love. My body actually trembled. Rock fans and critics have been misinterpreting this feeling for years — one of the clichés of the form is that a band or a song "changed my life." To them it means it launched the listener outside the bourgeois world of school and parents and into the world of antinomianism — and Democratic politics, if the politicians' affinity for rock stars is any indication. It's taken me a few years to figure out that these moments don't constitute change; they signal a reinforcement. They validate the idea that the supernatural world is real, and that even here in the vale of tears we can occasionally catch a glimpse of it. The night my knees buckled at "Under the Milky Way," I was not being a malevolent iconoclast thumbing his nose at the system. I was catching a fleeting glimpse of God.

> *"Become what you are." In the context of Powers's arguments, this seems to mean: become what you are when you are a fifteen-year-old.*

It's here that the fallacy about rock music as a progressive force is revealed. Rock is very simple, conservative music — which doesn't mean it can't be brilliant. The best rock can reach into the heart of beauty, which brings it in proximity with the divine. The connection between beauty and truth — and the truth of God — was examined by the theologian George Weigel in his book *Letters to a Young Catholic*. Weigel, in describing the Chartres Cathedral in France, notes that:

> Chartres is inconceivable without the obedience of faith. The people who built Chartres thought that they were building an earthly representation of the New Jerusalem — and perhaps "representation" isn't quite the right word. Those who built Chartres and those who gave of their substance to make Chartres possible believed that they were in the antechamber of heaven in this place. Chartres is uniquely a permeable "border" between the mundane and the transcendent, the visible and the invisible, the ordinary and the extraordinary, the human and the divine.

It is this border that I felt myself crossing that night I first heard "Under the Milky Way." I was an angry young rebel back in those

days, but the music I thought was a signifier of total freedom, indeed, anarchy, was a gateway to the orthodox truth that theologians
had known about for thousands of years. As Weigel points out,
"Beauty is something that even the most skeptical of moderns can
know. . . . People know that they know what's beautiful. Thus beauty
is one way we can introduce our doubting friends and colleagues to
the mystery they often deny: the mystery that there is truth and we
can know it."

— Chapter Six —

The Unknown Hoya

If there were any doubts left that Georgetown Prep in the 1980s had fallen far from the halcyon days of Archbishop Carroll, they were crushed when I took my first sex education class. It was taught by a man named Bernie Ward, a socialist who would go on to become a talk radio host in San Francisco.

On the first day of sex ed, Mr. Ward walked into the classroom, introduced himself, and passed out the text for the semester: *The Road Less Traveled*, the megapopular book of self-help dreck by M. Scott Peck. Then Mr. Ward made an announcement: "There is nothing wrong with masturbation."

We all looked at each other. Despite our growing up in the shadow of Woodstock, there was some primal, vestigial Catholic instinct left over from our parents. We suspected a trap. He was going to announce that there was nothing wrong with masturbation, see who laughed, and give the poor slob detention for a week.

"No, really," he continued. "Even if you're married. Not a thing in the world wrong with it."

He continued, telling us that in the next few months we would be learning some new terms: words like clitoris, vagina, ejaculation, penis, and others. Of course, we knew the words already. We had just never heard them in a Catholic school before.

Like all modern sex ed enthusiasts, Mr. Ward was a master of the incomplete truth. That phrase was used by the great twentieth-century theologian Dietrich von Hildebrand. In his book *Trojan Horse in the City of God*, von Hildebrand exposed a simple yet profound reality: we live in the age of the incomplete truths. As von Hildebrand saw it, an incomplete truth is just what it sounds like — something that is true, but not fully true. For example, if a Christian says that loving one's neighbor is the way to heaven it is true, but only incompletely. It's important to love one's neighbor, but only because such love glorifies God.

Von Hildebrand also applied his thesis to sex, admonishing the Catholic Church for regarding sex as simply and solely a way to procreate. (He wrote before John Paul II revolutionized the church's view of human sexuality with his philosophy of *The Theology of the Body*.) "The mystery of procreation itself can be adequately seen only against the background of the communion of love," he wrote. "The doctrine stressing procreation exclusively is an incomplete truth."

This doctrine is also one that stresses pleasure or body parts above the emotional and spiritual dimension. This is really, more than anything else, an attack on virtue. It was spearheaded in the twentieth century by Hugh Hefner and *Playboy* magazine, without whom it would be difficult to imagine Mr. Ward. The Catholic journalist and historian James Hitchcock has explored the way social mores changed due to Hefner. Before *Playboy* there were plenty of attacks on tradition morality (Hitchcock uses the lurid nineteenth-century magazine *Police Gazette* as an example). The difference was that whereas once people attacked the clergy for being hypocritical, not adhering to the immutable standards they preached, when Hefner came along the attack came to be on virtue itself. Those who claimed that virtue was a myth felt themselves to be more morally virtuous than those they were assailing.

Hefner outdid the Catholic Church, which once separated sex from love: he separated sex from both love and procreation. Hefner took sex and declared that it was perfectly natural and, as such, nothing to be ashamed of — really not all that different from going to the bathroom. As von Hildebrand noted, an incomplete truth is not a lie, which is why Hefner is such a slippery interviewee. Thrust with an argument about morality, and he parries with something that's hard to refute: sex is an normal instinct.

Yet the irony of Hefner is that he's missing out on the best sex in life, indeed the only sex that is human, that is, sex grounded in love of another person — or the only sex that is in fact a form of freedom. Sex is indeed natural. It also, as Hefner points out, often does not involve love. Yet when it does not involve love and is detached from shame — a healthy form of modesty — it is less than human and far less than sublime. Despite Hef's declaration that "we won" the sexual revolution, it is a victory without a prize. The racy *Playboy* lifestyle can now be heard panting as it tries to smile through AIDS, the depersonalization of the Girls Gone Wild generation, and the tragedy of oral sex among sixth graders. It is as empty and hostile to the individual person as the puritan chimeras *Playboy* has used as bogeymen for half a century. Hefner can tell his incomplete truth about biological needs and healthy sex, but he can't ignore the other half of that truth: sex is also supernatural, something that elicits a commitment from the soul and can be, in the words of John Paul II, "an icon of the interior life of God." Only an age as in love with irony as ours could produce the phenomenon by which the pope of the Catholic Church offers a more rich, mystical, realistic, and deeply human insight into sex than the world's best-known pornographer.

This, incidentally, is why the *Playboy* fiftieth anniversary issue, published in 2004, was such a bore. As the world emerges from the sexual revolution and tries to shake itself into a new sobriety, Hef is like the man at your fiftieth high school reunion who shows up with someone younger than your daughter and still tells those tired old "naughty" jokes. He never grew up, and the act is stale. He's still proclaiming the *Playboy* philosophy, a thicket of incomplete truths and outright lies: "We hold that man's personal self-interest is natural and good and that it can be channeled, through reason, to the benefit of the individual and his society." "The irony of censorship is that if we were to permit a completely unrestricted, censor-free society, none of the oft-expressed forebodings of social doom and moral degradation and disintegration would be realized." "We believe in the existence of absolute truth — not in the mystical or religious sense but in the certainty that the true nature of man and the universe is knowable, and the conviction that the acquisition of such truth should be one of the major goals of mankind." This kind of thing doesn't provoke outrage as much as sympathy: Can this old geezer

really still believe this stuff? That man's self-interest can do nothing
but good, that live sex on prime-time TV and prostitution in every
neighborhood would not cause trouble, and that religion has nothing
to tell us about absolute truths: these are the half-baked tenets of a
high school senior.

Even at Prep, our God-given instinct for the truth led us to realize
that there was something vulgar and comical about Mr. Ward, with
all his orgasms and ejaculations. He became a prime target for impersonation, and the herds of boys filing out of his class were more often
than not laughing. What was so sad is that in 1983, while Mr. Ward
was diagramming the female reproductive organs, Pope John Paul II
was offering his own sex education course. He was in the middle
of what would be 129 general audience addresses on human sexuality — what would become known as the theology of the body.
This was revolutionary stuff, an update and elaboration of *Humanae
Vitae,* the 1968 encyclical that rejected artificial contraception and
drove many Catholics to rebel. The theology of the body announced
a central paradox that the modern world never got: sexuality is of
far greater importance to Christians than the swinging modernist —
like Mr. Ward — could ever understand. Conjugal love between a
man and his wife was nothing less than "an icon of the interior life of
God." It was a holy form of self-giving and not to be treated lightly.
In *Witness to Hope,* his biography of John Paul, Catholic historian
George Weigel elaborates: "Few moral theologians have taken our
embodiedness as male and female as seriously as John Paul II. Few
have dared push the Catholic sacramental intuition — the invisible
manifest through the visible, the extraordinary that lies on the far
side of the ordinary — quite as far as John Paul does in teaching that
the self-giving love of sexual communion is an icon of the interior
life of God. Few have dared say so forthrightly to the world, 'Human
sexuality is far greater than you imagine.' "

In Bernie Ward's masturbation class, we didn't study the theology
of the body. The only philosophy we got was existential philosophy,
taught by a Jesuit named Father Macabee. Shortly after our graduation, Macabee would leave the order, come out of the closet, move
to San Francisco, and move in with a former student who had been a

year behind me. I didn't care, and don't care, about Macabee's homosexuality. I care about what he was teaching us, which had nothing
to do with Catholic humanism or Catholic philosophy. I point this
out because there were some outstanding teachers at Prep, and one
of them, who is gay, was a great help to me. I was a troublemaker
in school, and one year it got so bad that my name came out in a
faculty meeting. Some were worried that I would get kicked out before I graduated. A couple of days later one of my teachers, a gay
man, gave me a JUG detention. Normally JUG meant walking the
race track for three hours or sitting in study hall doing nothing, but
this time was different. The teacher put me in one of the classrooms,
and a couple of minutes later wheeled in a television with a VCR
hooked up. I thought he was going to make me watch some industrial
film about problem children or juvenile delinquency. It was a recording of the Royal Shakespeare Company performing *Hamlet*. He told
me he had read my papers, knew I loved Shakespeare, and believed
that I showed promise as a writer. My punishment was to watch the
performance.

---

*Even at Prep, our God-given instinct
for the truth led us to realize that there
was something vulgar and comical about
Mr. Ward, with all his orgasms and
ejaculations.*

Indeed, in subjects like English, history, and math the school had
teachers superior to any I had in college. They prepared us for college
in every way except spiritually. One history teacher I had taught
the subject in reverse chronology, starting with Watergate and then
moving back to Vietnam, the 1950s, and so on. He reasoned that
student were more interested in history that they remembered, and
he was right. This man is also a scholar in Catholic history and
has written several superior books on the subject. The school never
considered him a religion teacher — I guess because they didn't teach
religion.

Another great teacher there, Mr. Harry, taught English. One day our senior year he passed out index cards to the class. On each card was written a crime that had occurred in America over the past hundred years — murders, serial killings, unsolved mysteries. We had to spend six months in the university libraries in Washington — this was the days before the Internet — digging through old newspapers researching the case. Then we had to write a twenty-page paper about it. We were allowed only three typos on the paper, or we failed. The purpose was to teach us how to use the library and how to write, and it did both. I never forgot my case — H. H. Holmes, the serial killer in turn-of-the-century Chicago. I always intended to turn my paper into a book, but in 2001 someone beat me to it. *The Devil in the White City* became a bestseller. Many reviewers praised the author for digging up such an intense and forgotten case.

Prep also had an outstanding drama department that always managed to put on great shows despite having almost no budget and a much smaller talent pool to draw on than the larger public schools. One year they decided to put on *Grease* in the school gym, and we were all excited because the wealthy father of one of the cast members offered his Porsche for use in the "Greased Lightning" scene, where a character brags about the speed of his hot rod. Leading up to opening night there was talk all over campus about how awesome this scene was going to be, with the car actually being driven around to the front of the stage. At about two hours before show time the car arrived, silently curling up the long driveway to the campus. They pulled it up to the gym doors. Then they figured out that no kind of physics in the world could make that car fit through the narrow doors. They tried a crane, they pushed and pulled — they might have even prayed. The car was not going inside.

They turned this problem to their advantage. When the big scene came and the main character Danny was bragging about his car, out puttered an old golf cart. "That's it?" one of his buddies exclaimed. "It looks like a friggin' golf cart!"

Probably my favorite teacher at Prep was Father Hart. An ex-hippie who sported a short-cropped new-wave hairdo, Father Hart at once represented the worst excesses of the 1960s and a deep Franciscan mysticism. He loved Gandhi as well as C. S. Lewis. He taught religion, and his class often involved rock music. He printed out the lyrics to the Jimi Hendrix classic "Voodoo Child" and cranked the song on his little portable tape recorder. Another favorite was "Eminence Front" by the Who. Father Hart found all kinds of deep meaning in the song — the eminence front, he explained, was the phony face we presented to the world: the playboy, the big bad businessman, the prefect housewife. It denied our real humanity as fallen creatures.

Father Hart was skinny and of average height, and he sounded a little bit like Jack Nicholson. I didn't have his religion class, but we met one afternoon when he was supervising JUG. I was the only one in detention that day, and we got into a conversation about books and music. I was a huge fan of The Who, but I thought they had far better songs than "Eminence Front." What about "Bargain"? "Getting in Tune"? "Slip Kid?" Father Hart was a gentle person and — unlike the older disciplinary Jesuits and the younger ones filling us with propaganda — a good listener. And he was fascinated when I began to talk about *The Lord of the Rings*, my favorite book. He had never read it, but recommended *The Screwtape Letters*, the C. S. Lewis classic that he was using in his religion class.

After that Father Hart became a close friend. He did so despite the fact — or perhaps because of the fact — that he challenged us on a lot of the stunts we were trying to pull. One was the underground newspaper three of us put out. The official student newspaper, the *Little Hoya*, was so dull that I never had any interest in writing for it. It was a typical high school paper — straight news mixed with insipid editorials about parking problems and bad cafeteria food. There was also a sports page and innocuous features like "Student Spotlight" or "Faculty Profile," boring little pieces about a "noteworthy" student or teacher.

It was so bad that senior year, I, along with two other students, Brooke and a guy nicknamed "Slime," started an underground sheet called the *Unknown Hoya*. Although on the outside it was nothing more than a few mimeographed pages stapled together, the *Unknown*

Hoya, if I do say so myself, was a sharp and sometimes fall-down-funny paper. The best writer was my friend Brooke. He loved to do sections that stole from the format of the *Little Hoya,* and then used that format to ridicule a student. Thus, the *Little Hoya's* "Student Profile" of one of the overachievers in the school would become "Loser Profile" in the *Unknown Hoya,* celebrating the exploits of the student who was on probation. Brooke also came up with features like "Match the Student," where the reader matched the student in column A with the nickname in column B, and "The Latest Line," a list of "odds from Las Vegas" about certain students. That one kid known for making violent Claymation movies would wind up in an insane asylum: 3 to 1. Another who drank too much had a 1 to 1 shot of puking on New Year's Eve. That we all would graduate? 10 to 1. (He turned out to be right about that last one.)

Despite all its humor, however, it soon became clear that the *Unknown Hoya* was covering news that the *Little Hoya* would not. Most of it involved parties. The summer before senior year, the drinking age in Maryland had been raised from eighteen to twenty-one. Some guys in my class had made the deadline — there was a grandfather clause — but most had not. This left the Prep administration in an odd spot. It was legal for several seniors to buy as much beer as they wanted, and most of our parents, who had been used to the drinking age of eighteen, expected us to drink. Yet for most of us, buying and drinking alcohol was illegal.

Moreover, as I have written before, Prep was a school divided — between the few remaining old school traditionalists and the modern, liberal pedagogues who had come of age in the 1960s. The younger teachers and Jesuits were used to becoming friends with students and even drinking with them when the students turned eighteen. The older ones and a few of the younger ones felt that the raising of the legal age should spell the end of drinking at Prep altogether.

Despite the new law, the parties went on — with gusto. Senior year, my class of eighty decided that by the end of the year we would drink a hundred kegs of beer. The *Little Hoya,* of course, would never report on our progress, but the *Unknown Hoya* would.

We would also report on the bachelor party we threw for our music teacher. I'll call him Mr. Maud. Mr. Maud, like other teachers at Prep, was a hippie who had never left the 1960s. In class we learned how to read music, and our term papers were reports on our favorite rock bands. Mr. Maud was lanky, had a beard, and had a funny way of speaking — through his nose. He was ripe for impersonation, and I would imitate him at the slightest provocation.

Senior year, we threw Mr. Maud a bachelor party when he announced he was getting married. A guy whose parents were away volunteered his house, and we got a keg of beer and hired a stripper. We took pictures — of guys throwing up, drunkenly jumping into the swimming pool, mooning the camera. There were a lot of shots of Mr. Maud — chugging a beer, surrounded by a group of us with raised mugs, and sitting down while being entertained by the stripper.

We covered the party with a "pictorial essay" — i.e., several pictures pasted onto a few pages — in the *Unknown Hoya*. Under the picture of our music teacher staring the stripper in the chest, we couldn't resist adding the caption, "That's definitely not a B flat."

The *Unknown Hoya* also was the only paper to review *Derelict Death Wish*, a hilarious and deeply silly movie we made. It was directed by a kid in our class nicknamed "Fuzz." Fuzz was a genuinely talented filmmaker. He specialized in stop-motion movies done with Claymation, like the old California raisin commercials. He and a group of us decided to make a live-action epic called *Derelict Death Wish*. The plot was pretty simple: There was a kid in our class who looked exactly like Charles Bronson, and he would go around killing teachers. In today's post-Columbine age this might sound chilling, but if *Derelict Death Wish* was a disturbing revelation from demented minds, then so was *Gilligan's Island*. The entire thing was comic, a showcase for impersonation and slapstick much more than a gorefest. Indeed, it made the actors look just as foolish as the teachers. The word "amateur" just doesn't describe the final product. It made Ed Wood's *Plan 9 from Outer Space* look like *The Lord of the Rings*.

Still, it was something that took some effort. There were only two of us — my friend Brooke and I — playing all of our teachers. We had to dress like them, talk like them, walk like them. And we had to play the females as well. For the ancient, bald, and four-foot-eleven English teacher Mr. James, Brooke — the most talented — pushed his large head into a skin wig and walked on his knees (we shot him "walking" behind a car). For the hairy and hippy music teacher, I used three wigs — one for my head, one for each underarm. The headmaster, Father Howard, was easy — goatee and Buddy Holly glasses. We obviously couldn't use the classrooms, so we filmed outside with the school in the background. We set up desks we had "borrowed" to simulate the classroom. We wrote the credits on a chalkboard. The music was provided by the Jesuits, a rock band made up of four classmates, one of whom was in the movie.

When the final edit was complete, we had our grand premiere at my best friend Tommy's house in Bethesda, Maryland. It was a real movie night. We had about thirty people — both guys and girls — crammed into his living room. There was popcorn and beer. Fuzz set up, and we turned out the lights.

People went nuts. They were laughing so hard you couldn't hear half the lines. At the end they demanded to see it again and again — we had more viewings than *Titanic*. Of course, we gave the premiere full coverage in the *Unknown Hoya*. When the issue came out, I asked Father Hart what he thought about our movie and our paper, and he just shook his head. "You guys have what could be a great thing, and you're turning it into garbage."

I was offended. Slime, Brooke, and I were working hard putting the paper together, and on the days it came out we could see students all over campus tripping over themselves laughing. What was the problem?

Father Hart then went on a long ramble about the underground press in the 1960s, how it was not only satirical but stood for something. It hoped to achieve certain dreams and goals, like civil rights, when all we wanted to do was tear things down. To us, everything was a joke. We had no concern for the truth. We were mocking people without pointing to what we found good — aside from drinking, sex, and violent homemade movies. Hart was partially right. Perhaps we could have been more serious. But isn't there a kernel of seriousness to satire? In one issue of the *Unknown Hoya*, I editorialized against the school policy of censoring any pictures or references to alcohol in the yearbook — an unexpected change of policy that took effect our senior year. After a lot of jokes and cheap shots at teachers, I argued that if God had the same policy we would never have heard of the wedding at Cana, much less the Last Supper.

Prep was a school positively swimming in alcohol, and my class partied with gusto — often right under the noses of our teachers. During my junior year at Prep, three other guys and I decided to pull a stunt at the homecoming football game. Sometime in the 1970s Prep had lost its female cheerleaders, girls from Catholic schools in the area, because they had been humiliated by Prep boys in the bleachers making crude remarks. (It says something about Prep that it was the cheerleaders rather than the boys who had left.)

One afternoon I came up with an idea: we would be our own cheerleaders. The old girls' cheerleading outfits were still tucked away in a back room of the gym. We would put them on and form a squad for the homecoming game against Landon, another boy's school in Maryland. There were only four uniforms left, and I had no trouble finding three other guys to go along with the prank. There was only one imperative: we had to be drunk. There was no way we were going to storm the field during the homecoming game dressed in women's clothes if we were sober.

We got a case of beer before the game. We found a deserted lane near the school, and before the game we sat there listening to the Who and chugging beers. We each put away six, then dashed across the campus to the gym, which was next to the field. By the time we got to the uniforms the beers had hit us. We started giggling, each of us squeezing our legs into those tight navy blue skirts and clingy sweaters with the white stripe down the sleeve. Part of our uniform was white boxer shorts, and each of us had a word written on the backside so that when we lined up and mooned the crowd it carried a message: BEAT LANDON PREP #1.

The first quarter was already well underway when we burst from the gym and sprinted for the Prep sideline. I will never forget the reaction as the fans noticed us: they went insane. They rose almost as one, whooping and screaming at the return, after all those years, of

Prep's cheerleaders. We ran in circles, climbed the back of the bleachers, led cheers, and formed a pyramid that we were too hammered
to complete. It was obvious to everyone, including the teachers, that
we were drunk. Yet this was the post-1960s, pre-twenty-one-years-
old-to-drink Prep, so many weren't sure what to do. At one point
the history teacher, Mr. Oats, by far the most hostile to teen drinking, tried to say something to one of the guys as he scaled up the
back of the bleachers. The kid just shook his head and headed back
down the bleachers as he saw Oats approaching. Then we did our
underwear trick. "Gentlemen," I shouted, "assume the position!" We
lined up, did an about-face, bent over, and let the crowd have it.
Unfortunately, in our state we messed up the order. Our butts read
LANDON #1 BEAT PREP.

They did, too.

The next day Mr. Oats asked me to stay after history class. He
came up very close to my face. "I have just one question," he said.
"Was your enthusiasm at the game yesterday fueled by a foreign
substance?" I lied: "No," not out of shame, but of fear.

The tradition of the male cheerleaders has continued to this day
at Prep, although it's a lot more dull. In 2003 I was at a game there
when I noticed something odd: a group of about twenty guys, a few
dressed in the old girls' uniforms, gathered under a tree near the
field. After the game started, they all snaked their way in a line
to the bleachers. The uniforms, however, were different. They had
the skirts, but the tops had been replaced with Hawaiian shirts. I
couldn't help but think that the gathering under the tree and run to
the bleachers was an echo of our trip from the gym — sans the beer,
of course.

What Mr. Oats didn't appreciate was that what we did was a show
of school spirit, and that there was nothing wrong with having beer
to enhance the moment. The problem, of course, is understanding
such things in the context of the cardinal virtue of temperance and
how it worked. Temperance is discussed by Josef Pieper in his book
The Four Cardinal Virtues, another volume that should be on every
Catholic high school reading list. In it Pieper does what too many

Catholic writers in the modern era have had to do — reclaim the potency of the very language of morality.

Pieper notes that the very meaning of temperance "has dwindled miserably to the crude significance of 'temperateness in eating and drinking.'" Pieper insists that temperance, or *temperantia*, does not have to do with diminishing the passions; indeed, in the *Summa Theologica* anger is defended. "The current concept of moderation," Pieper writes, "is dangerously close to fear of an exuberance." This "emasculated concept of moderation has no place in a doctrine which asserts that the love of God — fountainhead of all virtues — knows neither mean nor measure." Rather than reject eating, drinking, and sensuality, Pieper sees them as pointing to the very essence of the human being. Yet these things must be done in the knowledge that self-fulfillment without God is not possible. Pieper adds:

> It is a noteworthy fact . . . that almost all pathological obsessions, witnesses as they are to a disturbed inner order, belong to the sphere of *temperantia*: sexual aberrations as well as dipsomania, delusion of grandeur, pathological irascibility, and the passive craving of the rootless for sensations. All these petrifactions of selfishness are accompanied by the despair of missing the goal striven for with such an exertion of will — namely the gratification of the self. For it is a natural, primal fact, prior to all human decision, that man loves God more than himself, and consequently that he must of necessity miss his very goal — himself — by following the ungodly, the "anti-godly," path of selfishness.

This is why intemperance and despair are linked: if one seeks perfect happiness in the pleasures of sex and other appetites with no knowledge of God, one's life will ultimately not be heaven but an "artificial paradise . . . of forgetfulness, of self-oblivion." While sin is "a burden and a bondage," temperance is "liberating and purifying." This purity, observes Pieper, is often attained "when the shock of a profound sorrow carries [man] to the brink of existence or when he is touched by the shadow of death." This sobriety brings purity, or purification, which allows one to open up to accept the love and grace of God.

If I wasn't learning Catholicism at Prep, I was from my dad. In the summer of 1982, my father took the family to Ireland. He and my mother had fallen in love with Ireland when they had first gone in 1980. They had gone back about every other year since then.

Dad became an Irish nationalist as a result, and a couple of times took the family to our ancestral home to teach us our history. He developed a deep antipathy toward the English, or rather toward the dead English who had tortured and suppressed the Irish. It was not the grudge of a dilettante who romanticized his Celtic roots; Dad did the research, and what he found was not pretty. He said as much in his 1981 piece in *National Geographic*:

> Two hundred years after Patrick's death [in the fifth century], Celtic Ireland was thick with monasteries, and Irish monks went out to France, Germany, Switzerland, and beyond, where they founded monasteries that kept the learning of Rome alive; in-deed, the Middle Ages may be said to have begun with the arrival of Irish monks at Charlemagne's court.
>
> The Irish have kept ever since the faith of Patrick, to their pride and sometimes to their utmost misery. I voice this sen-timent out of an American-Irish background with a standard symmetry of emotion: the wearin' o' the green on St. Patrick's Day, living shamrocks and cardboard leprechauns, 'Oh, the days of the Kerry dancing,' the priest with immaculate hands reading the Mass for the Dead while old women in black keened and rains from the wrong side of the Atlantic swept the streets of Boston, Baltimore, or New York.

One of the most interesting figures Dad spoke about was James McAuley, a Dublin contractor. Since at least 1695, it had been against the law to teach Catholicism in Ireland. That was the year the English, who had conquered Ireland — which was 80 percent Catho-lic — instituted the Penal Laws. Catholics were not able to hold public office, bear arms, or enter a profession. Priests were hunted and often executed. Catholics were often stripped of property, and courts made it easy for a Protestant to seize a home that belonged to a Catholic. "Our literature is rich in portraits of what it was like to be a Jew in Germany in the late 1930s or a black in America in the 18th and 19th centuries," journalist John Fialka wrote of the period. "To be a Catholic in Ireland in the later part of the 18th century was not far from that, measured in pain, poverty, and risk. But it is a story that many Irish Americans have tended to blot out of their memory and literature in their rush to assimilate."

The main point of the Penal Laws was not necessarily death, however, but conversion. It was illegal to teach children Catholicism. If a young man converted, he immediately became manager of his father's property. As a result many Irish went underground to keep their faith. They had "penal walks" where they shared the faith, had guarded "Mass fields" where they had services, and operated "hedge schools," classes held on high ground so jailers could be seen coming. Edmund Burke described the world created by the Penal Laws as the worst "contrivance for the impoverishment and degradation of the people . . . as ever proceeded from the perverted ingenuity of man."

Against this totalitarianism — and the abysmal poverty that went with it — stood a few resisters of particular bravery, among them James McAuley. McAuley was one of the luckier Irish: his talents as a house builder had allowed him a degree of acceptance among the English, and he enjoyed a middle-class life in Dublin. Yet he was willing to risk it all for the simple act of bringing dirty street children into his home and teaching them Catholicism.

McAuley's passion was inherited by his daughter, Catherine. In 1804 Catherine, twenty-six, was taken in by a Quaker couple. Catherine had inherited her father's compassion for the poor and was soon taking the family's carriage into the slums of Dublin, picking up the poor and hopeless, and bringing them back to a small house on the property where she worked to feed, comfort, and teach them. Catherine's employers were so impressed that when they died she was left the estate — worth an estimated one million in today's dollars.

She used the money to open a house for the poor. Eventually she would become a nun and form her own order, the Sisters of Mercy. The Sisters of Mercy would come to America and found schools all over the country — including Our Lady of Mercy in Potomac, Maryland, where I went to grade school.

Perhaps not surprisingly, we were never taught the story of the order that was responsible for our school. While James and Catherine McAuley had risked their lives to catechize Irish children, in my generation teachers were moving heaven and earth to prevent students from learning the faith. But there was a sign of hope. My senior year at Prep, the Vatican announced that it would begin work on the new *Catechism of the Catholic Church*. Cardinal Joseph Ratzinger (later Pope Benedict XVI), the prefect of the Sacred Congregation for the Doctrine of the Faith, gave a speech bemoaning the terrible state of catechesis. He called it "a grave error" when Catholic leaders and teachers declared that "the category 'catechism' was obsolete." Ratzinger reminded the audience that "from the earliest times of Christianity there appears a permanent and central 'nucleus' of catechesis, hence of formation in the faith." Ratzinger told of a German woman whose son was in a Catholic elementary school and had never heard of the seven sacraments or the Apostles' Creed. The most basic components of faith were being neglected. Some things were not neglected, however. Our goal of drinking a hundred kegs by graduation? I'm sorry to say that we succeeded.

Indeed, the night we drank our hundredth keg is illustrative of how far we had fallen from our parents. For most of the year we had had our parties at houses where the parents were away — including a disastrous one at my house where the place was trashed — but at the end of the year there was a graduation party with the parents and the teachers, including the Jesuits. It was held at my friend Donny Kane's house, a Maryland mansion complete with a pool and tennis courts. Donny's father had made it big as a lawyer, and their parties were legendary for their opulence — kegs of the best beer, waiters, tables filled with shrimp, caviar, and chocolate-covered strawberries. Despite their wealth, Donny's family was completely without pretense. They were known for their generosity to Prep and the local church, and would be the first to help a kid out who was in trouble. Their house was the safe spot to which we would all retreat to spend the night after a party. But even the Kanes weren't ready for the graduation party.

The plan was that the parents would have the inside and the kids the outside area of the pool and tennis courts, but as midnight passed and people drank, the invisible barrier broke down. Donny had eight younger brothers and sisters, and they were all showing off doing flips off the diving board. Soon there was a ring of about fifty people — parents, teachers, and Jesuits — around the pool and applauding each dive. My best friend Tommy, who, like the rest of us, was drunk, decided to do his own dive. He was a great athlete and football star at Prep, and a powerful swimmer.

> *While James and Catherine McAuley had
> risked their lives to catechize Irish children,
> in my generation teachers were moving
> heaven and earth to prevent students from
> learning the faith.*

A hush fell on the throng as he took a running start from the grass, suddenly breaking from the shadows into the pool floodlights. He took off from the cement, sank onto the board for what seemed like several seconds, then catapulted up and out like a cannonball. Then, in one graceful motion, he turned his body, squeezed into a ball, and snapped his bathing suit down to his knees to moon Father Howard, the headmaster of Prep.

At last, the two cultures, and the two generations, had clashed. While we all fell down laughing, the parents were mortified — and furious. Tommy's parents marched up to him and told him "get in the car, now." As the party broke up, with parents ordering their kids into the back seat for a silent ride home, there was one last indignity. Sex teacher Mr. Ward was walking through the front yard when he noticed movement behind a tree. He walked over to find a Prep student in a compromising position with a girl from Stone Ridge, the ritzy local Catholic girls school. Ward, not knowing what to do when confronted with the fruits of his teaching, simply tried to beat a retreat to his car. But the Prep student called after him. "Nothing wrong with masturbation," he yelled, "but this is a hell of a lot better!"

— *Chapter Seven* —

Catholic U.

It would be a stretch to say that I was a *student* at Catholic University. Technically, I was enrolled there and graduated from the institution in 1990 — seven years after graduating from Georgetown Prep. But I was never really there. I never lived on campus, instead boarding in various houses and apartments with Prep buddies.

Working on the *Unknown Hoya* at Prep and seeing my father traveling around the world for *National Geographic* had decided my future: I would be a journalist. In that regard, I thought college would just get in the way. Dad had warned me against going to journalism school, advising me to become an English major and read as much as I could. He always believed that anyone who went to journalism school was a hack.

Catholic University has had ups and downs in its history. One positive point is that it boasts the most beautiful campus in Washington. It's home to the National Shrine of the Immaculate Conception. In all my years at Catholic U., I, like many of my peers, never set foot inside the shrine, one of the most fantastic churches in the world. A small city of marble and stone, it combines Byzantine and Roman architecture and houses more than sixty chapels and oratories, as well as two churches — the upper church and the crypt church — and an underground chapel inspired by the underground spaces that persecuted Christians of the early church used for prayer and Mass. There are mosaics and statues depicting the Blessed Virgin from cultures all over the world. A person could spend a year in the shrine and not discover all of its treasures.

Like the rest of the church, in the twentieth century Catholic University had moved from a repressive conservative orthodoxy to a repressive liberal one. The change had begun in the postwar era and reached a peak in the late 1960s. In 1957, clerics and religious made up 41 percent of all full-time students. In 1966 that number had dropped to 29 percent. The rector of the university from 1957 to 1967 was Father William Joseph McDonald, a native of Kilkenny, Ireland. McDonald soon ran into trouble with some members of the faculty—specifically some members of the American Association of University Professors (AAUP). The chapter of the AAUP at Catholic U. had largely been considered independent of the administration, but McDonald changed this, going to the trustees to get prior approval for any speakers the AAUP had on campus. McDonald refused the AAUP permission to co-sponsor a symposium on evolution. He also had conflicts with the students. When the Catholic Student Mission Crusade wanted to invite a Buddhist to speak about the United Nations, McDonald nixed the idea. In 1963 a group of priests who were graduate students invited Jimmy Hoffa to speak on campus; McDonald apologized to Attorney General Robert Kennedy. When the Vatican asked Catholic university for recommendations regarding the upcoming Vatican II session, McDonald did not include recommendations from the faculty of the school of canon law. That same year he banned four liberal theologians from speaking on campus.

Things changed. While I was at Catholic U. in the 1980s, our most famous professor was Charles Curran, who was ultimately forbidden from teaching as a Catholic theologian. Curran had been controversial since his appointment to the faculty at Catholic U. in 1965. Newspapers reported that he advocated a change in the church's teaching on birth control. When the dean and the rector of the university spoke to Curran about it, he referred them to his book *Christian Morality Today*, which had the imprimatur of the bishop of Fort Wayne, Indiana. The University then formed a board to determine exactly what Curran's views were. Upon review, the board decided, effective August 31, 1967, that Curran would lose his position as assistant professor of theology.

The faculty of theology went on strike. They refused to teach until the chancellor had Curran reinstated. Curran went on to become a key dissident in the turmoil at Catholic University following

the 1968 encyclical *Humanae Vitae*. The night before the encyclical
was issued, a group of theologians at Catholic University, including
Curran, prepared a lengthy dissent. As a result nineteen Washington priests were disciplined by the local archbishop, Cardinal Patrick
O'Boyle. In April 1971, however, the Vatican's Congregation for the
Clergy issued a document calling for O'Boyle to remove the sanctions
he had imposed. O'Boyle, who, along with Pope Paul VI, wanted to
avoid controversy, removed the sanctions.

> *I was standing there lecturing Curran's
> foes about the curriculum, and I wasn't
> even much of a Catholic anymore.*

What became known as the Truce of 1968 had broad repercus-
sions for the church. Dissident priests and theologians now felt that
they could disagree with the Vatican about major issues without
paying a price. As church historian George Weigel put it, "Theologians, priests, and religious men and women under vows of obedience
could, in effect, throw a Papal encyclical, a solemn act of the
Church's teaching authority, back in the Pope's face — and do so with
impunity. The culture of dissent, professional division, was born."

Father Curran would ultimately run afoul of the magisterium and
be refused the right to teach as a Catholic theologian. This happened
in 1987, while I was at the university. Curran's teachings on abortion,
birth control, homosexuality, and sterilization had become too liberal,
even though Curran claimed his position fell under the category of
"faithful dissent." Nonetheless, Curran was banned from teaching as
a Catholic theologian.

In the midst of the fight, I attended a press conference held by Curran at the university. When the question-and-answer period came, I
raised my hand and launched into an editorial disguised as a question. I had been educated by Jesuits, I announced, who had taught
us about contraception and sex. There had been no problem then, so
why the problem now? Curran said I had made the point precisely.

Looking back, I can feel only embarrassment at my stupidity and arrogance. What made it ironic was that I was standing there lecturing Curran's foes about the curriculum, and I wasn't even much of a Catholic anymore. Freed from the mandatory Masses of Georgetown Prep, I'd stopped going to Mass. My heart hadn't been in it since my days at Our Lady of Mercy, and it wasn't difficult to see why. I hadn't been assigned the Bible or any decent theology in twelve years of Catholic schooling. I hadn't been assigned a single papal encyclical on sex or any other topic, I couldn't name three saints, and I didn't know how to pray, yet I felt qualified to pontificate at a press conference — and then to write an editorial defending Curran for the school newspaper the *Tower*. This would be like editorializing about the history of jazz music without knowing the names Louis Armstrong, Count Basie, Duke Ellington, Ella Fitzgerald, John Coltrane, and Wynton Marsalis.

Even as the Curran episode was garnering headlines around the world, most of the students at Catholic U. didn't seem to care. We were post–Vatican II Catholics, which meant we weren't so much liberal as just plain ignorant and oblivious. One student, however, wasn't ignorant — Paul Julio. Julio was known and derided around campus as a mirthless conservative crusader, defending the faith against the drunken infidels who had come spilling out of post-1960s America. Julio wrote editorials condemning Curran and the entire campus ministry department at Catholic U. Yet Julio had one thing on his side that his enemies did not: the facts. Julio knew his stuff. He had read the Vatican II documents and most papal encyclicals. When he wrote attacking Curran, he was inevitably met with a blizzard of angry letters, but as Julio himself noted, none of them was bolstered by actual facts.

Indeed, a lead editorial in the *Tower* went so far as to celebrate this very ignorance. "What might the uninvolved or less passionate advocate make of all this fuss over Campus Ministry?" it asked.

One perceives quite clearly two sides defending their "turf."
Both sides perceive themselves as true ministers of the Word.
And one also perceives a vast number of those who could care

less while conservatives battle liberals. What happens to those who could care less? Might not the battle of conservative versus liberal be said to create that uncaring middle? And who ministers to that group of students who don't see the merits of either side and who see the dispute as a serious condemnation of the church itself? Come down from your pulpits, all ye faithful; the uncaring stand ready to destroy you!

In other words: "There's no such thing as truth — so why the fuss? It's the fighting itself that causes apathy." This is brain-freeze logic that wouldn't have made sense even at Woodstock. They were right about one thing, though: the kids at Catholic U. certainly were apathetic. But it wasn't an apathy of the scholar who reached it on the far side of theological reflection and study. It was the apathy of the idiot.

I met Julio once, at a meeting of staff and writers for the *Tower.* Not being apathetic, but indeed being an idiot, I called out to him, "So you're that fascist who writes those editorials!" I soon realized I was no longer in the Prep family, where busting on people was sport and everyone gave and took freely. Julio, a small, skinny guy with glasses, shrunk away from me. The room fell silent. I felt like a jackass. If I could find him today I would apologize. Julio's editorials still hold up.

Despite people like Father Curran, there were some outstanding teachers at Catholic U. Two of the best were a nun, Sister Anne, who taught Shakespeare, and Professor Hagan, who taught a course called "New Journalism." I didn't know it when I walked into Caldwell Hall that cool September night in 1984, but Professor Hagan was about to change my life. There were about four of us in the class. Hagan was a tall, wiry man with thick glasses. He was very soft-spoken. That first class he gave us the syllabus: books by Tom Wolfe, Hunter Thompson, Gay Talese — the so-called "new journalists" of the 1960s, men who abandoned the dull old journalism to write with a more literary flair. I got my new books the next day, and in the afternoon opened up the collection of Tom Wolfe's essays. I started reading, and didn't stop until about 4 a.m., when I had read the book straight through. Here was the kind of journalism I wanted to do: literary, opinionated, even brash. Honest and funny.

Our main assignment in the class was to simply write a story and try to get it published. Hagan was the first to tell me what I now tell young aspiring journalists: send your stuff to the *Atlantic, Rolling Stone,* the *New York Times,* and the *New Yorker.* Now. Why wait? I remember we all looked at each other with shock when Hagan told us we would be sending our articles to these cathedrals of journalism. But why not? What could it hurt? I choose to do a piece on punk rock. I still remember how my piece started — with the sentence, "They're out there tonight." I spoke of the punk rockers who hung out in Georgetown and other places in Washington while their parents and the more conventional were asleep. I interviewed a girl I had known growing up who had gone punk, and some of her friends.

Toward the end of the piece I ran out of enthusiasm, and the story lost focus and passion. I remember Hagan reading my piece in front of the class, delighting at how good it was — for the first half. "You kind of dropped off a cliff near the end," he said. He was right. I cleaned up the ending, then sent it out for publication. It got rejected, but I received encouragement from an editor at *Rolling Stone.*

Hagan knew that even the most rule-breaking writing needed a stable, coherent base to thrive. This is where Sister Anne came in. The single most memorable and rewarding class I took at Catholic U. was her Shakespeare class. She had — and still has — a mastery of the subject and an enthusiasm that is contagious. One of the funniest parts of the class would be when we were studying a passage that had heavy sexual overtones — or outright bawdiness. Sister Anne would hem and haw, blush, clutch her chest then finally blurt, "Well, I think we all know what he means here!" She also has a wonderful sense of humor.

I also developed a crush on Miss Stunts, Sister Anne's assistant. She was a pretty young English woman who helped grade papers and taught when Sister Anne was out. In 1985 Miss Stunts encouraged me to enter an essay contest the school was holding. The topic was how and why to alleviate the African famine that, thanks largely to the Live Aid rock concert, was then in the news. Here's where the lessons I learned in the New Journalism class took over. Rather than try to impress the judges with my deep empathy, I wrote exactly what I felt: the entire essay contest was a sick exercise in liberal guilt. Its only purpose was as a showcase for how much empathy the writer had for the suffering. A better essay, I offered, would examine how the famine had happened. Inspired by Wolfe and Thompson, I blasted the judges as a bunch of hippy-dippy do-gooders. On the day they announced the winner, I was in a bar in Georgetown getting drunk. I called Miss Stunts, not to see if I won but to see if I was in trouble. I had come in second. I remember standing there holding the phone, stunned.

Second? How did that happen?

I then learned one of the most important lessons in journalism: say what's in your heart, say what you're passionate about, and forget about what is expected of you. Doing what is expected of you means covering Little League soccer for the *East Peoria Sleeper* for the rest of your life. Bolstered by alcohol, I asked — well, it may have been closer to begging — Miss Stunts to come down and join me for a drink. It was a pure Holden Caulfield moment. She seemed flattered — and embarrassed — and politely turned me down.

While I did write many embarrassing things for the *Tower* while at Catholic U., there was one piece I'm still proud of. One night I was in a bar with some Prep friends when one of them — I'm happy to say, someone who was not a close friend and who had gotten kicked out of Prep — started talking about how gross and filthy and unnatural homosexuality was. It was around this time that my brother Michael was making his way as an actor, and I had gotten to know his friends, many of whom are gay. The next day I wrote an editorial about what had happened and said that as Christians we are called to serve those with AIDS no matter how they got it. It's probably the best thing I wrote while at Catholic U.

It wasn't the piece that generated the most mail, however. That honor went to the editorial I wrote about Bruce Springsteen. I've never been able to stand Springsteen, with his faux populism, working-class-hero shtick, and cheesy New Jersey ballads. In 1985 his megablockbuster album *Born in the USA* came out, and his face was everywhere. It's been said that the capital of New Jersey is Catholic University because the school has so many students from there. I wrote a piece for the *Tower* dubbing the Boss a talentless hack. It got so many angry letters — one from my own brother — that they had to expand the Letters page. For several weeks I was terrified to walk across campus, ready to get my ass kicked at any minute. Years later, I would again launch an assault on the Boss, this time in the pages of the *Wall Street Journal*. The hate mail again came pouring in.

My New Journalism class and Sister Anne's Shakespeare were the two bookends framing my writing career. You could write with honesty and sarcasm, but it only worked if you had one foot in structure and tradition. It would not have been possible without these two professors. (Hagan is long gone, but I was delighted to see Sister Anne again in the spring of 2003. She appeared at the CUA bookstore where I was doing a signing of my book *Damn Senators*.)

These classes provided the excitement that could have come from theology classes. But sadly, the few religion classes I took at Catholic U. were mostly terrible. The one required religion class was taught by a hippy named Professor Dirges. Dirges delighted in pointing out the contradictions in the Bible — as if as Catholics we read that book literally in the first place. He would stand in front of the class, read a passage, then flip to another that contradicted it. "That's a *contradiction*, folks!" he would cry. Everyone shrugged. So what? Another religion course I took encouraged us to explore every faith except Catholicism. For our final paper we had to visit the place of worship of another faith. I decided to go the Hare Krishna compound in Potomac, the town where I had grown up and where my parents still lived. I stopped by home to pick up some supplies from Dad — a tape recorder and camera. Dad, the ever-serious intellectual, thought the idea was great. I made some crack about wasting time with bald-headed airport hustlers, and he chided me. "Don't be a jerk. You're a journalist representing Catholic University. Try to learn something."

I must admit it is something I never forgot. Potomac is a wealthy suburban area, and it was jolting to go from cul de sacs with nice suburban lawns and homes to this camp with spiritual seekers jumping up and down. I went through the ceremony with them to get the full effect. I only wish I had been equally immersed in the richness of Catholicism. To paraphrase Chesterton, I had to set out to discover my own land.

It was around the time of Curran's press conference that my dad became internationally known, at least for a brief period of time. As mentioned earlier, in November 1986 he published, in a cover story for *National Geographic,* the results of a story he spent years working on: the actual site where Christopher Columbus had landed in America. For decades historians believed that Columbus landed on San Salvador, a small island in the Bahamas. According to my dad, however, the scholars who made that claim had not taken into account the effect of wind and currents in driving the *Niña, Pinta,* and *Santa María* slowly south over the course of the journey. Using computers to account for the effects of wind and current, Dad drew a track that led to another island, Samana Cay. He led an expedition down to the island, where within an hour of landing they found buried remnants of old Spanish pottery from the fifteenth century.

For several weeks, Dad was in every newspaper and all over television. The phone rang from reporters several times a day. Scholars whose work he had debunked furiously called for debates. A press conference at *National Geographic* attracted so many reporters it had to be held in an auditorium. A fan bought Dad a ten-foot Columbus statue-cum-birdbath, which we erected in the backyard. The high point came when my dad and several editors from the *Geographic* were invited to the White House to meet President Reagan. Dad was an old-school FDR Irish Catholic Democrat, and no fan of Reagan's. The White House provided him with two copies of a photograph of Dad shaking hands with the president; one was signed by Reagan at the bottom, the other left blank. Dad wrote on the blank space, "To Ronald Reagan, best wishes, Joe Judge," and hung that one up in his den.

The Columbus coup was also one of the few times my dad got really angry with me. One of his journalist friends made Dad a copy of a thirty-second tape of baseball manager Tommy Lasorda delivering an aria of obscenities after a particularly bad loss. At the height of the Columbus media frenzy, my mom and dad decided to get away for a week-long vacation. On the day they left, I thought it would be funny to put the Tommy Lasorda tape on the answering machine. Then I went to a party one of my Prep buddies was having. After having too many beers, I had to stay overnight and didn't get home until late the next day. When I got home there were five messages on the machine — four from bewildered reporters from CBS, CNN, NBC, and the *Washington Post,* and one from my dad. He was not happy, but my dad was incapable of staying angry for long. When they got home from vacation he tried to lecture me but could not keep a straight face — especially since my older brother was there and kept muttering, "Best prank ever."

It was around this time that I discovered that peculiar feature of post–Vatican II life, the CINO journalist — Catholic in Name Only. I was working in a record store when I met a man named Bob Hulteen, who liked the same music I did. He was an editor at *Sojourners,* a magazine based in Washington, D.C., and founded by Jim Wallis, a liberal Christian preacher. The main emphasis at *Sojourners* was on helping the poor, particularly the inner-city poor. The office was near Catholic University, in a building that had once been a dormitory for prospective priests.

It took Bob and me only a few minutes to become friends, and he asked me to write some record reviews for the magazine. I met and became friends with the rest of the staff and was amazed at the depth of their commitment to Christ and to the poor. When they prayed before a meal, they really meant it, closing their eyes tight and avoiding rote prayer in favor of a more personal conversation with God. Jim Wallis is the most soft-spoken preacher I've ever met. Sometimes when he spoke, I had to lean in close just to catch what he was saying.

I was so taken with them that I even decided to go with them to Mass — or to what they considered Mass, a kind of faint echo of the Catholic liturgy I had grown up with. It was held in a small building in inner-city Washington, a space that doubled as a day-care center. I had always been taught to face the cross when receiving communion, and when the moment came at the *Sojourners* service I received the bread — from a female "priest" — then stepped away to face the cross. I didn't see it, so I turned to another wall. This continued until I had done an entire 360 and realized there was no crucifix. My friend Bob just laughed. "We took him off the cross," he said. "You Catholics have Jesus up there all bloody. We put him in heaven."

While the staff at *Sojourners* were personally living out the gospels with a self-giving commitment that eluded — and still eludes — me, in their pages I discovered many of the Christian writers who espoused liberal Christianity. The Catholic ones were people like Rosemary Radford Ruether, Garry Wills, and E. J. Dionne. Particularly in the days before the new catechism was published in 1994, these Catholics could sell basically anything as Catholic dogma. A favorite trick is the "seamless garment" argument, which held that to be pro-life means that protesting against war and advocating health care is as important as fighting abortion. In fact, my old parish and school, the very liberal Our Lady of Mercy, is a big fan of the seamless garment argument. One church bulletin advises followers of Christ: "Weave the seamless garment of a consistent life ethic whose fabric consists of all the principles of Catholic Social Teaching."

In one *Sojourners* article, Tom Allio, the senior director for the Diocese of Cleveland's Social Action Office, puts it this way: "To be pro-life means also to work to eradicate poverty, to provide universal health care, to provide affordable housing, to be consistent on war and peace."

To the Catholic Church these issues do indeed form a seamless garment, but in a hierarchy. The *Catechism* explains just war theory and the belief that in some cases the death penalty is justified. There is no such complexity when it comes to abortion. "Formal cooperation in an abortion constitutes a grave offense," it says. A person who procures an abortion "incurs excommunication *latae sententiae,* by the very commission of the offense." It is "a crime against human life."

Can the same thing be said for someone who supports the war against terrorism, or doesn't support single-payer health care? Not according to the *Catechism*. So instead of pointing to the church's official teaching manual, the Catholic Left, well, lies. It's also worth noting that, as the late theologian Frank Sheed noted in his book

The Church and I, Christ's words against the rich always emphasized the harm that obsession with wealth does, not to the community but to the soul of the rich person himself. "It was not for the exploitation of the poor" that Christ attacked the rich, Sheed wrote, but "of only thinking of this world and not the next; as Christ puts it in Matthew, for 'laying up treasures on earth where rust and moth consume, instead of in heaven.'"

Dionne, Wills, and other liberal Catholics are also good at marshaling St. Francis of Assisi to their "progressive" causes. Has there ever been a saint as sentimentalized as St. Francis of Assisi? The very sight of the popular iconography of Francis, surrounded by animals and flowers, brings a warm Disney feeling that plays well in parishes like Our Lady of Mercy, schools like Georgetown Prep, and magazines like *Sojourners.* He was the man who loved nature, the world's first environmentalist — and who could be against that? Stop in any garden center in America to buy flowers, and there he is in stone. Yet in his book *Francis of Assisi: Performing the Gospel Life,* University of Notre Dame professor Lawrence S. Cunningham hoses the treacle off the great man. Cunningham does so with soft, quiet deliberation and a very simple strategy: relying on the facts.

The most important of these is that St. Francis followed the gospel, a basic idea that has been lost. Simply put, Francis fell in love with Jesus Christ and took his words to heart. Far from being a leftist (Cunningham notes that Francis has been co-opted by at least one Communist, Antonio Negri), Francis was an orthodox Catholic. Francis grew up spoiled in the mercantile class of Assisi, a town about a hundred miles north of Rome. After a wasted youth he had a conversion, whose exact time and place is not documented, based on Christ's interaction with lepers. There followed what Cunningham refers to as "other conversions" into a deeper understanding of the gospel — most notably the move to absolute poverty. Over the years Francis was turned into an iconoclast protesting against the authoritative church (particularly in the nineteenth century and now in the postmodern West). Yet Cunningham notes how Francis was following many of the rules from the Vatican, and emphasizes that the saint's love of nature was based solely on the world as a gift from God.

Very few people, even those with St. Francis holding watch over their garden, know that Francis suffered from stigmata, the wounds of Christ, later in his life. Cunningham realizes that this was not an aberration, but the fulfillment of a life of faith: "Anyone tempted to sentimentalize the saint needs to recall that his life from his youth to his final years forms a great inclusio [single theme] bracketed by the Crucified One."

Alan Keyes: "If the barometer of the church's health is teenagers in Mass, we're in more trouble than I thought."

Many liberal Catholic journalists lecture and write about social justice and what's wrong with the church, but never answer a very simple question: whether or not they truly believe in Jesus. James Hitchcock once noted that in the 1960s liberal Catholics asked questions about the liturgy, proper dress, contraception, infallibility — everything except the question of whether they had faith. They never discussed whether they believed in Jesus. Indeed, many Catholics define their Catholicism by the leverage it gives them in the liberal culture. They have a double game going: they can earn points for being pro-abortion and gay rights at cocktail parties and in editorial meetings, while maintaining insider status as members of the church. It's like helping to beat your brother to death and then claiming immunity from prosecution because it's a private family squabble.

"My church is in trouble," Dionne warns in an indignant column about the sex abuse scandal — this from a writer who has never, at least in all the columns of his I've read over ten years, praised the name Jesus Christ in print. He's never even burnished a papal encyclical. On CNBC Mike Barnicle sees the storm clouds gathering because teenage boys are giggling in Mass. (This inspired the brilliant rejoinder from Alan Keyes: "If the barometer of the church's health is teenagers in Mass, we're in more trouble than I thought.") To Dionne, the church doesn't represent joy, the eternal, or even love; it's simply a piñata to string up whenever church teachings don't conform to the latest liberal fad. Garry Wills, a *Sojourners* favorite, has made a career out of scalping the church because it won't give in to his demands for contraception and female priests. I've never read a word Wills has written about how he genuinely feels about Jesus Christ.

One suspects that at heart many of these journalists are political utopians, rejecting the Christian idea of redemptive suffering or even holy sorrow. This seems especially true of E. J. Dionne. Dionne once eulogized a friend, the liberal priest Monsignor Phil Murnion, who was "an organizer" — meaning he was involved in liberal causes. Dionne offered high praise:

> What occurs to me is that the trajectory of [Murnion's] life, in the church and in the world, centered on hope inspired by the civil rights organizers and by the movement for renewal in the Catholic Church embodied in Pope John XXIII's call for the Second Vatican Council. Hope is different from optimism. Hope is a tough virtue, not a psychological disposition. Hope insists on taking facts and reason into account and still insisting that improvement — along with, if you are religious, salvation — is always a real possibility.

Dionne managed to get the meaning of hope exactly wrong. Maybe it wasn't on purpose. Maybe he really is that religiously illiterate. More likely, he's blinded by ideology, which, as was the case with me when I was younger, *is* his religion. Dionne ties the theological virtue of hope to liberal social progress, an attitude that is part of secular religion. Again, Josef Pieper offers some clarity. Pieper wrote an entire book called *On Hope,* but his sharpest summation of the virtue came in an essay called "The Obscurity of Hope and Despair" that ran in the German journal *Tradition als Herausforderung* in 1963.

In this essay, Pieper explains that both despair and hope have become "obscure," that is to say, have lost their true meaning. Despair, he explains, is really a product of sloth — sloth, that is, in the true meaning of the word. Sloth isn't laziness per se, but the failure to raise oneself above animal instincts and the urge to chase utopian dreams — the kind of dreams Dionne and those on the Left are lost in — to embrace one's true nature as a spiritual being, albeit a being in a world where evil can drive us backward and there is no guarantee of progress. "Through the sloth that is sin," writes Pieper, "man barricades himself against the challenge handed to him by his own dignity. He resists being a spiritual entity endowed with the power to make decisions.... In other words, man does not want to be what he nevertheless cannot stop being: a spiritual being, truly satisfied with nothing less than God himself; and beyond that, 'son of God,' rightful heir to eternal life." Without this belief one is left with "the immense effort of a forced optimism, of a radiating trust in life, of a noisily proclaimed 'progress.'"

In other words, what Dionne calls the "tough virtue" of hope is actually a way to the despair of a false utopian optimism. Dionne ties hope to liberal social progress, which can in fact be what Pieper refers to, quoting Heidegger, as an "opportunity to abandon oneself to the world." Pieper goes on to elucidate what separates secular from Christian ideas about hope. While both have the sentiment that things will turn out all right in the end, "Christian hope, however, cannot be separated from certain concepts about the structure of the world of history. And this is the reason that this hope, in the extreme case, can take on so much of the nature of obscurity that to the eye of the non-Christian it is nearly unrecognizable and comes to be seen almost as despair. This idea of the world of history, the world of humanity, says... that evil possesses power in this world, going even so far as to say that evil, seen from a standpoint inside the world, may appear to be the superior power."

This is not to say that there is no such thing as a "natural hope," and that man should not attempt to right wrongs in the world. Pieper notes that "one can call anyone blessed" who devotes himself to social causes and the health of his family. Yet this is not reflective of the true nature and ultimate destiny of man, whose being points to salvation: "Man is not set in the 'true inner order' simply because he hopes for a happy old age or for the well being of his children or for peace on earth or even that humanity may be saved from destroying itself. ... Hope only becomes virtue as theological hope... meaning a hope moving toward salvation, which does not exist in the natural world."

It would not be accurate to say that Christian hope rejects the world. Indeed, Christian martyrs are careful not to fall prey to "a supernaturalism excluding history or to a pure activism within history or to a tragic attitude that is fatalistic and hostile to creation." Yet the holy goodness of earthly creation is temporary. and subject to destruction by the forces of evil.

To Dionne and to so many other liberals, the march of human "progress" embodied in Vatican II and the civil rights movement makes up the essence of the virtue of hope itself. Hope can exist only if the world keeps moving in the right direction.

Another Catholic journalist and utopian — who also has very little to say about Jesus — is Andrew Sullivan. In 2004 Sullivan, who is openly gay and won't rest until the church changes its position on homosexuality, wrote a piece for the *New York Times*. It was revealing about the narcissism of the modern liberal Catholic and exposed the total illiteracy of the secular press in terms of transcendent moral values, God, and how they relate to human action. On Sunday, May 30, 2004, the *New York Times* ran two pieces in two different sections that nonetheless complemented each other perfectly. The first one reported, in dispiriting detail, the problem of teenage promiscuity in America. The second piece, a celebration — indeed, a sacramentalization — of sex, was an unintentional example of how that very problem of promiscuity came to pass.

The first piece, "Whatever Happened to Teen Romance?," appeared in the *New York Times Magazine*. Journalist Benoit Denizet-Lewis, who had spent a great deal of time with a group of American teenagers, reported to the liberals who read the *Times* the same news conservatives have been heralding for years: our children are out of control sexually. Monogamy is a joke. Hook-ups, that is to say, sexual encounters without strings, are in — as is "friendship with benefits," meaning having a friend with whom you can have ongoing sex without any emotional commitment. And oral sex is common among kids as young as ten.

The second piece was Andrew Sullivan's review of Tony Hendra's memoir *Father Joe: The Man Who Saved My Soul*. In the review, Sullivan can barely contain his joy. *Father Joe* is about a Dominican priest who became a mentor to Hendra, a writer and actor perhaps best known for playing the part of the band manager in *This Is Spinal Tap*. They first met when Hendra was caught having an affair with a married woman whose husband (a "hyperstrict Roman Catholic," of course) sent her to the priest. Father Joe taught Hendra many things, but the most notable to Sullivan — who is himself obsessed with sex while always claiming that the Catholic Church is — is the idea that sex is a sacrament and that his affair is not really a sin.

To Father Joe, Hendra's problem was no problem. The point of sex is to give pleasure as well as receive it; as long as one does that, everything is cool. As Sullivan puts it,

> Tony's sin was not the groping or the lust as such but the sub-jection of a "hungry, trapped, unhappy woman" to his own narcissistic pleasure and needs. Father Joe, in one swoop, both undermines the current hierarchy's obsessive horror of sex itself and illuminates the real point of Catholic sexual ethics: the re-spect and love for another human being made in the image of God.

Later Father Joe elaborates that sex is "almost like a sacrament." Hendra, shocked, asks if the priest is saying that sex is a sacrament. "Don't tell the abbot!" Father Joe replies. Hendra presses on, de-manding to know if Father Joe is claiming that sex is not a sin. Father Joe: "Sex is a sin less often than we're led to believe. It's all a question of context. If you have sex to hurt or exploit another, or to take pleasure only for me, me, me, and not return as much or more to your lover . . . then it becomes sinful. . . . We must take the fear out of sex as well."

One would have to hire the entire staff of *Playboy* magazine to come up with sentiments that more perfectly summarize where we've gone wrong sexually. Sex is at once holy in and of itself — no need to get God involved — and coldly utilitarian. What is so distress-ing and so frustrating is that the Andrew Sullivans — and Father Joes — of the world, far from being libertines, are actually shackled by their childish and limited perception of sex. In Sullivan's philos-ophy, sex is not about losing yourself completely in the desire for a loved one; that is, for the entire loved one as a person (Pope John Paul II recognizes this in his massive *Theology of the Body*, a book Sullivan never mentions). There's none of that wonderful freefalling where you seem to cease to exist, and all that's left is God and his incredible gift, your beloved (for us "hyperstrict Roman Catholics," that means your spouse). Instead, moral sex is about mechanics. It means giving as well as you got. Talk about taking the mystery out of something beautiful.

And what a tragedy. The sex-ed utilitarians are helping destroy one of the last grand freedoms and adventures postmodern man has left. Losing our fear of sex, as Father Joe councils, is like seeing one of those behind-the-scenes specials about your favorite movie: once you know how every trick is done, you can't watch the film with the same thrill anymore, and even begin doubting any film's ability to transport you. In his *Times* piece, Denizet-Lewis offers two observations and joins them with a telling conjunction. The sexed-up teens he interviews "talk about hookups as matter-of-factly as they might discuss what's on the cafeteria menu — and they look at you in a funny way if you go on for too long about the emotional components of sex. *But* [my emphasis] coupled with this apparent disconnection is remarkable frankness about sex, even among friends of the opposite gender."

That the demystification of sex would go hand-in-hand with a casual frankness — i.e., the loss of feeling — would not be a shock to anyone but a *New York Times* reporter. Thirty years ago the connection between the two was made by Josef Pieper in his book *On Love.* Decades before Hendra's affair, Father Joe's Club Med catechism, and Andrew Sullivan's narcissism, Pieper warned against treating sex as a sacrament — of confusing a gift from God with God himself.

> There seems nowadays some strong imperative to conduct our-selves as though eros really were a kind of absolute authority. There are those who feel that they are right, are carrying out a kind of religious duty "in the service of eros" — even though they may be deceiving a spouse, betraying a friend, abusing hos-pitality, destroying the happiness of others, or abandoning their

own children. Then everything appears as a "sacrifice" painfully
offered upon the altar of love.

Pieper then quotes C. S. Lewis, who said that "When natural things
look most divine, the demonic is just round the corner."

Lewis also said that "natural loves that are allowed to become gods
do not remain loves." They become demons and destroy themselves
and those who worship them. This seems to be what is happening
with our children's loss of love. This was brilliantly explored by Pieper,
who was sadly prescient in *On Love:*

> Human personality forbids being used for the ends of others. Yet
> in consumer sex, which deliberately fends off love, the partner is
> regarded purely as a means and instrument. Hence the human
> face is not seen at all (this ignoring of the other may be quite
> mutual). Complete absence of human warmth is almost requi-
> site. Consequently, in such a detached sexuality there is hidden,
> despite all the outward show, a measure of frigidity in the clin-
> ical sense of the word. There is also, insofar as the relationship
> of person to person is concerned, an element of violence and a
> tinge of exactly the same "totalitarian coldness" which pervades
> the atmosphere of dictatorships and of purely technocratic so-
> cieties — in which there is no room for the "green thing" called
> love, so that again the human being is driven to the seem-
> ingly open but, in fact, deceptive escape route of isolated sex
> consumption.

After writing a few articles for *Sojourners* and graduating from
Catholic University in 1990 — my fondness for bars and rock and
roll had caused me to take an extra three years to get my diploma —
I began to get other freelance assignments as I worked retail and
restaurant jobs. I even came to the attention of the *Washington Post.*
In 1989 I had sent them a long letter protesting an article about rock
and roll and the death of political activism in post-1960s America
and was asked to meet with two of the editors. One of them took me
to lunch at the tony Madison Hotel across the street from the paper

and told me he wanted me to start writing some op-ed pieces about "anything you want."

Shortly thereafter, a local paper sent me to interview a teacher at Archbishop Carroll High School near Catholic University. Let's call him Richard Smith. Even among the liberal Catholics of Washington Smith had gained a reputation as a left-wing bomb thrower. He turned out to be the personification of everything that had gone wrong with Catholic education after Vatican II.

I walked into his classroom on the morning of Thursday, January 17, 1991 — the dawn of the Gulf War. The first thing I noticed was that the lights in the room were not on. Thirty students entered and took their seats in semidarkness. The blinds had been drawn; a lone candle burned on the corner bookshelf. Verdi's *Requiem* swelled out of a portable tape recorder. From framed photos on the wall, the faces of three dead martyrs gazed down at the fidgety sixteen-year-olds: Robert Kennedy, Martin Luther King Jr., Mitch Snyder. And, since this was a Catholic schoolroom, Jesus Christ gazed down at them too. Only this Christ was bearing a cross made of missile warheads.

Smith, standing at the front of the room, quietly greeted the class. Then, without warning, he grabbed a knob on the tape recorder and cranked up the volume until the music was a throbbing din.

"What's a requiem?" he shouted at his class.

In the back corner of the classroom, a kid's hand shot into the air. The student shouted something inaudible below the swelling chords.

"*What's that, Chad?*" bellowed Smith — turning up the volume another peg. "*What's wrong with you? You've got to learn to speak up. I can't hear you!*"

Chad screamed his answer back, but nobody could hear a word he was saying. Everyone started to laugh.

"A requiem Mass," Smith told the kids, turning his back to scrawl the word on the chalkboard, "is a Mass for the dead."

Smith then urged his students to share what they really thought about the first U.S. war they had ever known. "Please don't be afraid to take a position different from mine," the preppy-looking Smith chummily invited, "even though I will launch into you."

A chubby, round-faced kid named Darrius took him up on the offer. "I thought that the war was necessary," volunteered Darrius. "It had to come sooner or later, and better sooner than later on."

"Did you watch George Bush's speech?" Smith wanted to know.

"Yes, I did. And I . . ."

"Yes sir," Smith whined bitterly, "and you sucked it up like a dry sponge."

"It was good," Darrius pleaded, but the room had erupted in shouting — a test-tube *McLaughlin Group* with Smith's shrill wail rising above the din.

"You bought it!" he shouted, "Go! Sign up! Go! Go! Fight for freedom!"

Darrius held his ground and waited for the mayhem to die down. "If you refuse to go now," he insisted, "and they defeat us over there, they're going to come here next."

"Yes, I can see them!" Smith mocked, moving to the window, zipping a blind open and peering into the parking lot. "Look, here they come!" The room exploded with laughter. Smith turned back to face his target. "It's amazing. He only had a twelve-minute speech, and he got you. You actually watched him do that with all those stupid expressions on his face, and you still bought it."

"You make the same expressions," quipped Darrius, and everyone laughed again.

A tidy Pennsylvanian with strawberry-blond hair, well-ironed shirt, tie, and khakis, Smith was a Vietnam vet who cared deeply about children and, despite his occasional sarcastic bluster, was one of the most gentle people I've ever met. He was also a dangerous ideologue and propagandist who should not have been teaching high school. Smith grew up in Erie, Pennsylvania, in what he called "a very straight, Catholic upbringing." In 1970 Smith enlisted in the U.S. Army and volunteered for duty in Vietnam because he was "bored." He studied Vietnamese for three months in Texas and was shipped out as a lieutenant, arriving as part of the 22nd Advisory Corps assigned to a South Vietnamese army unit, where he was one of just two American GIs. Smith's tour ended in 1971. Smith's mind was expanded but not altered. He resolved to help cure poverty and human misery by becoming a priest; aspiring "to be the pope and solve all the world's problems in five years," he joined St. Mary's Seminary in Baltimore. There he became a legend — not for his dogged rebellion, but for his orthodoxy: "I was still for the war. And people would argue with me in seminary, down at the pub. And I wasn't equipped. I would tell the same anecdote over and over again about the president of South Vietnam planting rice in my village. And if he can do that then we're on the right side."

Fellow seminarians, he recalled later, "would go to their friends and say, 'You have to go down to the lounge 'cause there's this lunatic talking about rice.' And they would say to me, literally, 'You are f***ed up. You are *f***ed up.*' And I had no answer for that."

Smith was one of the most gentle people I've ever met. He was also a dangerous ideologue and propagandist who should not have been teaching high school.

Smith soon became a radical, however. Things in Vietnam went sour, and he began to rethink his position. Then he saw a movie, *Montgomery to Memphis*, on the mission of a peace activist about whom Smith knew precious little: Martin Luther King.

Smith went into teaching. But instead of droning on about the Trinity, transubstantiation, and the Immaculate Conception, he shared his views about Vietnam, King, and the U.S. labor movement. To him, teaching religion was teaching rebellion — with Christ as the ultimate rebel.

"If I'm supposed to be teaching Christian morality," he told me, "the teaching of Jesus, which side am I supposed to give? Am I supposed to give an evenhanded approach: Well, Gulf & Western puts it this way, and Jesus puts it this way, and you pick and choose what you want? I never believed that Jesus counts among his friends multinational corporations or the Donald Trumps of the world. The Gospels clearly sided with the poor." Then he offered this: "The major theory in the class is that we're all in a process of evolution. From green slime paramecium towards this being of the future, God only knows what it is, but we're not yet there" — he drew a semicircle on the blackboard with arrows marking our incipient progress — "but we are going to get there."

In me Smith was preaching to the choir. Oh, I didn't believe in Jesus anymore or any of that Catholic crap, but I was willing to manipulate it to political ends. Like Smith, I was willing to engage in all kinds of half-truths. In my entire interview with Smith, the Vietnam vet never once mention Communism, Pol Pot, or the boat people — or any of the other disasters that had happened to Vietnam after the United States pulled out. He praised Dorothy Day's service to the poor but never mentioned her anticommunism or orthodoxy. He never mentioned the word "abortion." He claimed, and I believed, that we were not helping Kuwait drive the invading Iraqi army out of their country. In short, rationality had no place here.

Shortly after I interviewed Smith, I ran into one of my old friends from Georgetown Prep in a bar. I began telling him about Smith, and then I lectured him about how evil Republicans, America, and Catholics are. He looked at me calmly — the Prep guys can see right through B.S., especially mine — and calmly asked me a question: "Tell me, Mark, what is your idea of a perfect world?"

I just looked at him. "What?"

"You're God," he said. "You can do anything you want. Tell me what you would do."

I just sat there. He had me. I realized that, like the liberal Catholic journalists, I had a list of things to complain about but not one positive thing to offer. How could I? The Immaculate Conception, the divinity of Christ, the Holy Spirit, Thomas Aquinas, Dietrich von Hildebrand, G. K. Chesterton, St. Thérèse — that was all the great stuff about the Catholic faith, the faith that makes sense of the world, and I knew nothing about any of it. Like the Western intellectuals in the early twentieth century who excused Stalinism not out of any sound philosophy but out of sheer hostility to the human mind — hostility to thought itself — I couldn't abide any reasonable, rational argument about the real nature of the world, God, and human beings. I was ready to destroy the world and build another one, but I had no idea what I would do differently — except maybe get rid of all the Republicans and religious nuts, and change human nature while I was at it. Like most atheists I didn't disbelieve in God — I hated him. I hated him because I refused to accept: that in the very weaknesses of my human nature was the key to freedom; that the suffering and stupidity of the world was to be experienced as a sharing of the passion of Christ and turned into something good; and that in that transformation was the ultimate answer to the meaning and purpose of the human person.

Cardinal Joseph Ratzinger (Pope Benedict XVI), one of the most brilliant theologians in the church, knew my type all too well. I was one of the radical utopians who, when they take their utopianism far enough, become totalitarians and terrorists. It was a particularly toxic problem when combined with the drug explosion in the 1960s — the decade that was formative for so many liberal Catholics. In his book *A Turning Point for Europe?* Cardinal Ratzinger draws a link between terrorism and drugs:

> Terrorism's point of departure is closely related to that of drugs: here, too, we find at the outset a protest against the world as it is and the desire for a better world. On the basis of its roots, terrorism is a moralism, albeit a misdirected one, that becomes the brutal parody of the true aims and paths of morality. It is not by chance that terrorism had its beginning in the universities, and here once again in the milieu of modern theology, in young people who at the outset were strongly influenced by religion. Terrorism was at first a religious enthusiasm that had been redirected to the earthly realm, a messianic expectation transposed into political fanaticism. Faith in life after death had broken down, or at least had become irrelevant, but the criterion of heavenly expectation was not abandoned: rather, it was

now applied to the present world.... Disgust at the intellectual and spiritual emptiness of our society, yearning for what
is completely different, the claim to unconditional salvation
without restrictions and without limits — this is the religious
component in the phenomenon of terrorism.

I wanted to destroy the world. Instead I was destroying myself.

— Chapter Eight —

Twelve Steps to Man

I suppose it should be noted for the record that after I graduated from Catholic University — and indeed even years before — my bar-hopping lifestyle caught up with me. There are far too many self-serving drunkalogue books out there, including my own, so there's no need to go into personal detail. I drank too much and did stupid things. That's my story. Besides, I was led back to the church through reason and grace, not through alcohol or the swearing off of alcohol.

While I don't want to dwell on the nastiness of alcoholism, I do feel compelled to say a few things about Alcoholics Anonymous as it relates to the Catholic Church and Christianity in general. I would not have stopped drinking without AA. Yet I have not stayed in the organization. In many ways the liberalization that happened to the church over the last forty years also has happened to AA.

As the very founders of that organization frequently emphasized, the point of AA is to get alcoholics back into circulation with the rest of humanity and to have a spiritual awakening that did not have the self as a godhead. AA cofounder Bill Wilson put it well: "Sobriety is just the beginning." To too many twelve-steppers, however, sobriety is the be-all and end-all of life. They can be so focused on their meetings and their "program" that they cannot see, and have no interest in, any greater things, much less what Pope John Paul II calls "the shattering mystery that is Jesus Christ."

Moreover, many AA members can see absolutely no good in their old lives as users. In their zeal to repudiate their old lives they tell a lie, that absolutely no part of life as a drinker has any value. To be sure, the lies, waste, and destruction that are all part of a life of an alcoholic are sins to be regretted. But this should not be taken to mean, as it often does, that no good comes from a drinking life. I know drinkers who have more zest and exuberance about the wonder and goodness of God's creation than many religious people I have known. The Prep parties, the riotous weekends at the beach, the sore jaw from staying up all night laughing, the magic of a first kiss after nerves have been eased by a couple of beers, the hilarity of my family at Thanksgiving, my father drunk and laughing so hard he couldn't deliver one of his horrible jokes — these are thing you don't hear about in AA meetings. Yet I think God put alcohol in this world for people to have fun with it — provided they also understood the virtue of temperance.

In the 1980s, before I stopped drinking, my favorite Washington pub was in a two-hundred-year-old building that had been a house. A trip there meant camaraderie, laughs, conversation spanning every conceivable topic, great music, and the possibility of love. In their own way these are all expressions of joy, of the joy that comes with existence.

Of course, without temperance all of this can turn into sin, as I discovered. I escaped that hell after graduating from Catholic U., thanks largely to AA. What I would ultimately discover, and tire of, is the organization's anti-Catholicism. A member of Alcoholics Anonymous will tell his story, and inevitably there will arise what I call "the Catholic moment." The person will reveal that he was raised a Catholic — or a Protestant or Orthodox Jew — but never knew God until he got into AA. Not that he has anything against Catholics, mind you, it's just that — well, there are all those rules, or the nuns who hit him with rulers, or, as one older gentleman bluntly put it in one meeting, "organized religion sucks."

Indeed, the primary role of the Catholic Church in AA is that of piñata. It's the one acceptable target in an organization that, rotten with liberalism and New Age blather, prides itself on acceptance of every conceivable kind of faith. This is a shame but not surprising, considering that one of the most remarkable Catholic priests who ever lived, a man who played a vital role in the origin of AA, has been all but forgotten even in the rooms of AA itself.

His name was Father Ed Dowling. He was a descendant of Far-rell Dowling, who had been exiled to Connaught, Ireland, in 1654 by Oliver Cromwell. A compulsive smoker and overeater who suf-fered from crippling arthritis that forced him to use a cane, Dowling understood suffering — although by all accounts his ebullient sense of humor and love of baseball made him a joy to be around.

Dowling would get from his living quarters at St. Louis University to his office at Queen's Work hospital several miles away by standing in the middle of the street and whistling. He would arrive at work some days in a limousine and others on a garbage truck. "He had a good time on both rides," one witness said. In November 1940, Dowl-ing, who was not an alcoholic, became interested in the then-new program of Alcoholics Anonymous. The organization was only a few years old and struggling. It had been formed when Bill Wilson, a New York stockbroker and alcoholic, had had a religious experience in a hospital while trying to dry out. Alcoholics Anonymous was a pas-tiche of Jungian psychology, which emphasized the values of religion in working wonders where science failed; Christianity lifted from the Oxford Group, a nineteenth-century evangelical group that sold ac-tivism; and the then-progressive medical theory that alcoholism was a disease. The foundation of AA was, and is, the now-famous Twelve Steps, which encourage followers to admit they are alcoholics, list all of their faults and share them with another human being, pray and meditate, have a spiritual awakening as a result, and "carry the message" to other alcoholics.

In those early days, the going was rough. Wilson was broke, very few alcoholics he tried to help were getting sober, and thousands of copies of the Big Book of AA that he had written were sitting in a warehouse unsold. On a rainy night in November 1940, Wilson was lying in bed on the second floor of an AA club on Twenty-fourth Street in New York when his wife announced a visitor. When Wilson heard a slow, limping shuffle, he sighed. Another drunk coming to pester him.

The visitor was Father Ed Dowling, using a cane because of his arthritis. Dowling introduced himself. "A Jesuit friend and I have been struck by the similarity between the AA Twelve Steps and the

Spiritual Exercises of St. Ignatius." "Never heard of him," Wilson replied. Dowling roared with laughter. Then he started to talk. The effect he had on Wilson was recorded later by Robert Thompsen, Wilson's biographer:

> Bill could feel his body relaxing, his spirits rising. Gradually he realized that this man sitting across from him was radiating a kind of grace that was filling the room with a strange, indefinable sense of presence. Father Ed wanted to talk about the paradox of AA, the "regeneration," he called it, the strength out of total defeat and weakness, loss of one's old life as a condition for achieving a new one.

Dowling spoke of suffering as a paradoxical path to holiness. As Dowling would later put it while quoting Whittaker Chambers, "And yet it is at this point that man, that monstrous midget, still has the edge on the Devil. He suffers. Not one man, however base, quite lacks the capacity for the specific suffering which is the seal of his divine commission."

That night Wilson opened up to Dowling, doing a fifth step — admitting your wrongs to another human being — with the priest. The priest encouraged Wilson in his work, often quoting Wilson's own language from the Big Book back to him. That night Wilson slept soundly for the first time in months.

The two men would become dear friends, and Dowling would become an important and much-loved figure in AA until he died in 1960. His name is nowhere to be found in virtually all the AA literature, with the exception of a book called *The Soul of Sponsorship: The Friendship of Fr. Ed Dowling, S.J. and Bill Wilson in Letters* by Robert Fitzgerald, S.J. The book offers a rich rebuke to modern members of AA who criticize the Catholic Church or other mainstream religions in meetings. Dowling once gave Wilson a copy of the *Spiritual Exercises* of St. Ignatius Loyola, and Wilson claimed to have been inspired by them while working on the book *Twelve Steps and Twelve Traditions*. Wilson was fascinated with the church but could never bring himself to convert to Catholicism. His primary problem was with the doctrine of infallibility. "It is ever so hard to believe that any human beings, no matter who, are able to be infallible about anything," he wrote. "There seems to be so little evidence all through the centuries that God intends to work that way."

Dowling responded that Wilson was right — human beings are fallible — but "a Power greater than ourselves" is not, and that Power can speak through human beings. When the church declared the doctrine of the Immaculate Conception, Dowling wrote, many found it "uselessly irritating." Then at Lourdes Mary declared herself the Immaculate Conception — "and then as now at Lourdes the blind see and the lame walk."

It's hard to understand why AA has let the memory of Dowling fade, but it would be of great service to the organization to reintroduce him. AA's origins in hard-core, Oxford Group Christianity have been watered down by the Oprah culture, although the problem may go even farther back than that. In his comprehensive book *Not-God: A History of Alcoholics Anonymous*, Ernest Kurtz notes that two conflicting impulses have been internalized in Western cultures — Enlightenment secularism and its reaction, Romanticism. "Thus," Kurtz writes, "in yet another paradox, moderns readily accept 'feeling' even as they resolutely reject 'belief.' "

This is the place AA finds itself in today. Like so much of our culture, it was to become narcissistic and detached from age-old traditions. Indeed, it is often openly hostile to some traditions, as I found out for myself. This is probably why there are virtually no Catholics like myself in the organization.

Yet Father Dowling points to a way out. In 1955 Dowling addressed AA at its twentieth anniversary celebration in St. Louis. He noted that AAs like to think of the Twelve Steps as humanity's steps to God, yet Dowling proposed that God had also taken twelve steps to man:

We know AA's Twelve Steps of man toward God. May I suggest God's Twelve Steps toward man as Christianity has taught them to me. The first step is described by St. John. The Incarnation. The Word was God and the Word became flesh and dwelt amongst us. He turned His life and His will over to the care of man as He understood him. The second step, nine months later, closer to us in the circumstances of it, is the birth, the Nativity. The third step, the next thirty years, the anonymous hidden life. Closer, because it is so much like our own. The fourth step, three years of public life. The fifth step, His teaching, His example, our Lord's Prayer. The sixth step, bodily suffering, including thirst, on Cavalry. The next step, soul suffering in Gethsemane; that's coming close. How well the alcoholic knows, and how well He knew, humiliation and fear and loneliness and discouragement and futility. Finally death, another step closer to us, and I think the passage where a dying God rests in the lap of a human mother is as far down as divinity can come, and probably the greatest height that humanity can reach.

Down the ages He comes closer to us as head of a sort of Christians Anonymous, a mystical body laced together by His teachings. "Whatsoever you do to the least of these my brethren so do you unto me...." "I was sick and I was hungry and you gave me to eat." The next step is the Christian Church, which I believe is Christ here today. A great many sincere people say, "I like Christianity, I just don't like Churchianity." I can understand that.... But, actually, I think that sounds a bit like saying "I do love good drinking water but I hate plumbing." And then the eleventh step is several big pipelines or sacraments of God's help. And the twelfth step, to me, is the great pipeline or sacrament of Communion. The Word that was God became flesh and becomes our food, as close to us as the fruit juice and the toast and the coffee we had an hour ago.

After I stopped drinking, I was able to focus more sharply on my journalism career. As I mentioned earlier, I was still writing for *Sojourners*, as well as left-wing magazines like the *Progressive* and *In These Times*. I got a day job at a bizarre magazine called *Common Boundary*, which had an office in a small house in Bethesda, Maryland. The magazine's motto was "The Common Boundary between

Spirituality and Psychotherapy." It was a journal that involved matters New Age, the neo-gnostic movement that was popular in the early 1990s. The staff of about ten people, headed by two ex-hippies, wrote articles about all things spiritual and therapeutic — that is, as long as those things in no way resembled orthodox Christianity. It was like a mix of Oprah, Timothy Leary, and the philosophy of Carl Jung. We covered Eastern mysticism, forms of meditation, the meaning of Jungian archetypes, healing from abuse, and "caring for the soul." The writers we profiled were huge bestsellers at the time but now largely forgotten: feminist Clarissa Pinkola Estes, men's movement doyen and poet Robert Bly (author of the bestseller *Iron John*), author and Jungian expert Marion Woodman.

Common Boundary's favorite Catholic was Matthew Fox, a radical priest who would ultimately be defrocked. Indeed, he was in the process of being kicked out of the church while I was working at *Common Boundary*. The magazine came out every other month, and it seemed like in every issue there was an update on Fox and his war with the Vatican. I should say that while the staff were against orthodox Catholicism, they were nice, respectful people; they rejected Catholicism on philosophical grounds, but unlike a lot of anti-Catholics, they had thought about it. When they criticized the Vatican, it wasn't shrill or angry, but based on some event or theological position. Moreover, they often let me write what I wanted to. I wrote about the Vietnam Veterans' Memorial, stylish African coffins, and alcoholism. I got to go up to Harvard to interview Dr. John Mack, a psychiatrist who treated people who believed they had been abducted by aliens. My dad had always been interested in UFOs, and when I got home he was waiting for the verdict.

"Well?" he said when I came through the front door.

"They're not nuts," I said.

While I don't think these people were taken by little green men, they were not lying. Something had happened to them. I just never figured out what. I knew enough to pad the article with a lot of New Age explanations about "transpersonal psychology," the "inner voice of the soul," and other claptrap.

I wouldn't last very long there. Even for a liberal, unserious Catholic like me, it just got too weird. Every year we would have a conference, "Care of the Soul," and I would wander from room to room in the hotel checking out all the action: people meditating, or intentionally making themselves hyperventilate to try to enter an altered state, or reading feminist poetry. I may not have been a Catholic, but I wasn't ready for the lotus position either.

While I was still at *Common Boundary,* Rome was preparing to issue the English translation of the *Catechism of the Catholic Church,* which had been issued in French in 1992. In liberal Catholic circles, there was a powerful effort to defang the catechism and even prevent its wide use. The English translation had taken two years because the initial translation had been heavy with politically correct language. The initial translator had been Father Douglas Kent Clark, a priest from Richmond Hill, Georgia. Clark had insisted on using "inclusive" language in the new catechism, changing words like "mankind" to "humankind" and refusing to identify God with the pronoun "He." According to Father Clark, "so-called inclusive language reflects a concern that is almost overwhelming in the United States."

Yet this use of inclusive language, along with other errors in translation, often altered the very meaning of the catechism. In a devastating critique of the translation in a 1993 *Crisis* magazine article, Msgr. Michael J. Wrenn and Kenneth D. Whitehead deconstructed the deconstructions of Father Clark. They noted that for over a thousand years the word "man" has been used in a generic sense to denote the entire human race. Moreover, inclusive language can wind up being exclusive; by changing "man" to "men and women," it leaves out children. Suddenly, Wrenn and Whitehead write, the Catholic faith "finds itself joined in a rather crude and uneasy mésalliance with a brand of feminist ideology that comes to us from the American Sixties." Perhaps most simply, changing "man" and "him" to the jarring "people" and "him or her" can make the catechism lose its rhythm, its poetry.

Wrenn and Whitehead offered dozens and dozens of examples of outright mistakes in translation. Many of them, intentionally or not, subverted Catholic teaching. Perhaps the most egregious was the passage where the catechism describes the Christian's "right and sometimes duty of making a just protest against that which may appear harmful to the dignity of persons and the good of the community." In the translation, the word "just" is translated as "lawful." In other words, the Christian is obligated to fight things that assault personal dignity, but only in a lawful way. As Wrenn and Whitehead point out, this would preclude protesting abortion in those countries where it is legal. Another passage reminds us that Christ's life is a mystery of redemption, including "in his Resurrection by which he justifies us." The translators changed this to "in his Resurrection because he justifies us." This is not a small difference, as it completely reverses Christian theology, making it seem as if the Resurrection resulted from our justification rather than the other way around.

I wouldn't last very long at Common Boundary. *Even for a liberal, unserious Catholic like me, it just got too weird.*

While Rome was trying to correct Father Clark's mistakes, a symposium at Catholic U. in 1993 was attempting to discredit the catechism before it had even been translated into English. Referring to the new catechism, Catholic U. theology professor Dr. Peter Phan announced that "to affirm *tout court* that 'the old law is a preparation for the Gospel' runs the risk of anti-Semitism." Phan claimed that in the new catechism, "while Vatican II is copiously cited, its spirit, as many commentators have lamented, is conspicuously absent." Citing "the spirit of Vatican II" is a classic trick used by liberals to refute anything about the church they don't like. They never get around to citing the *letter* of Vatican II, which robustly runs throughout the *Catechism of the Catholic Church.*

It was around this time that I finally landed an article in the *Washington Post*. Ironically, it had to do with Catholicism. Cable TV was just becoming widely used, but along with the advantage of a hundred channels came the propensity to sit in front of the screen for hours. I decided that I would fight the lure by giving up TV for Lent. Even though I knew nothing about Catholicism, I, like a lot of liberal Catholics, was more than willing to exploit the religion when it suited my purpose.

My article in the *Post* was the only kind of Catholic piece the modern media allows — light, funny, not defending orthodoxy or challenging liberal social mores. James Bowman, the brilliant media critic for *New Criterion* magazine, once noted that liberal bias in the media is not only manifest in how mainstream news outlets cover events, but in what they choose to ignore. Yes, snotty put-downs and downright editorializing appear in the news pages of the *New York Times* and the *Washington Post*. But what about the stories that simply don't get covered? This occurred to me in 2002 when I had returned to the church and was on the Catholic U. campus. The *Post* doesn't cover Catholic U. much, or even the neighborhood surrounding the school. CUA is in the heart of Brookland. Brookland, known to some as "Little Rome," is home to over sixty Catholic organizations and orders, including the Basilica of the Shrine of the Immaculate Conception (one of the largest churches in the world), the U.S. Council of Catholic Bishops, the Dominican House of Studies, the John Paul II Cultural Center, Carmelite and Franciscan monasteries, and Trinity College, a small and distinguished all-women's Catholic college.

It was also the place where some news was made during my visit, although the *Washington Post* and even the *Washington Times* missed it — probably because it happened during the same week as the protests against the International Monetary Fund, which were being covered literally every twenty minutes by NPR and the local media. The local television reporters were positively hysterical with anticipation of the protest, which consisted of a few hundred ill-bathed rich white kids ululating against the capitalist system that afforded them the cars they used to drive into Washington.

During my visit to Catholic U. I was walking to the university's Mullen Library when I was brought up short by two lines of graffiti that had been left on the sidewalk:

IT IS NOT SAFE
IT IS NOT RARE

As an alumnus I should not have been surprised that there is still a strong pro-life voice at the university, but still, I was brought up short. That kind of 1960s-style activism just wasn't routine at CUA. It hinted that there may have been a controversy at the school, and I ducked inside the library to get a copy of the *Tower*, the school paper where I got one of my starts in journalism. In fact, there was something of a fracas going on at the school — and in a world where leftism is *de rigueur* on campuses it was the kind of man-bites-dog story that should have filled the campus with reporters.

A rock band called Rusted Root had been hired to play at the school, but after the contracts had been signed and checks cashed, it was revealed that the band is a supporter of Planned Parenthood — indeed, that it often gives out Planned Parenthood literature at its shows. Students for Life protested, and the campus was in the middle of an intense debate about what to do. The pages of the *Tower* were filled with tough and thoughtful editorials and letters about the controversy. Many wanted to cancel the concert. "This is a concrete opportunity to reject an awful apathy towards an awful, pervasive reality," wrote Senior Terry Prosser, "a concrete opportunity to hold up the virtue of hope in the face of a monster. Hopeless you say? Did the end of slavery look so promising in 1820?"

Michael Tenney, a sophomore and member of the campus ministry staff, noted that Rusted Root had already been paid. He then came up with an idea: students with tickets to the show should show up wearing white T-shirts to symbolize their beliefs. "Wear white for life," Tenney wrote. His idea was supported by the forty-four hundred pink and blue flags that had been planted on the campus as a "Cemetery of the Innocents," a flag to indicate every abortion that happens annually in the United States.

The display, of course, attracted no professional reporters. After all, this isn't anti-apartheid shantytowns at Dartmouth. At the Rusted Root concert, there was not a single reporter from any newspaper present. The brouhaha lasted well into the following week, when the *Tower* ran several pages and an editorial on the controversy. The lead editorial actually defended Rusted Root, while most of the letters expressed outrage. It never occurred to the *Times* or the *Post* to do what newspapers in the old days did routinely — send reporters around the city, even (or perhaps especially) to places that seemed very quiet, and see if there was any news to be found.

This was how H. L. Mencken, perhaps the twentieth century's greatest newspaperman, got his first byline. Mencken was eighteen years old in 1899 when he began pestering Max Ways, the editor of the *Baltimore Herald,* for a job. Mencken showed up every night until finally one night Ways told Mencken to go to Govanstown, then a village north of Baltimore, to see if anything was happening. Mencken traveled through the aftermath of a blizzard to get there, and his description is one of the best passages from his book *Newspaper Days.* Mencken crossed "the glacier of a street" and woke an undertaker to ask for news, but the man had none. Then he went to the drug store, where he found "the druggist hugging a red-hot egg-stove behind his colored bottles." The druggist told him the town cop had just left to investigate the robbery of a horse and buggy. Mencken had a story and his first byline. Mencken was frequently sent out on such trips; Ways informed him that he would know he had traveled far enough out of Baltimore when he "ran into the reporters from Philadelphia."

Come to think of it, in my years at Catholic U. I don't recall ever — not even once — bumping into a reporter from a local paper. Never did I hear some hack say that he was there just to check things out, read the student paper, see what was going on. These days, most reporters, both left and right, miss the Catholic University story.

By the time I got to the *Post* it, like other major newspapers and like television networks, had begun simply pretending that most of the country is not Christian. In 2004 I decided to go back exactly fifty years and read the *Post* for ten days, from December 16 to December 26, 1954. I would then do the same for the same time period almost fifty years later, in 2003.

The results shocked even me, someone who already believed that the mainstream media ignores and belittles Christianity. For one thing, the 1954 coverage of Christmas was beyond anything I could have imagined. My initial plan was to skim each day's paper and make a copy of every Christmas-related article. I immediately realized this would mean copying about two-thirds of the paper. Christmas was simply everywhere. On the front page. In Sports. In the "City Living" section. In full-page photographic spreads. On the editorial page and in concert reviews. In the Food section. There was a two-page spread dedicated solely to religion, with a weekly column by Norman Vincent Peale. On December 16, the front page was already running the fourth in a series of features of "well-known Washington residents giving their personal reminiscences of the Christmas celebrations in foreign lands." The entry this day was by Dr. You Chan Yang, the ambassador from South Korea. Yang described the holiday in his home country, noting the Communist hostility to religion. Others in the series would include ambassadors from Ireland, Australia, and India. Apparently, in the 1950s multiculturalism meant that different countries had different traditions for celebrating the oneness we all share in Christ.

On December 17 began the Parade of Peace, a Christmas festival held — yes — on the National Mall, right across from the White House. No ACLU caterwauling here. The *Post* reprinted the "Pageant Program" for the festival. It included Christmas concerts, a speech by President Eisenhower, productions by the Boy and Girl Scouts, benedictions and a Mass with the Holy Cross choir, and a square dance followed by a "Catholic Holy Hours Service." All this on the National Mall. The paper also covered the Christmas celebration of regular folks around the city. The *Post* sponsored a month-long Christmas Homes exhibit, where certain families decked their homes out with Santas — live and plastic — and invited the public inside. There were Christmas tea parties and dances and luncheons and dinners. The *Post* reported the events, no matter how mundane. In fact, reading what you would expect would be boring facts about kids singing carols and getting dressed up and turkeys in the oven is a mesmerizing window into the spiritual energy of a real community. It's what journalism is supposed to be: unalloyed reporting on people, places, and things.

Yet what about the unrepresented? What about Jews, blacks, and unbelievers? Well, unbelievers and blacks are simply not present. Obviously in this sense the *Post*'s coverage is a failure. Worse, the "For and About Women" section is a cringe-inducing flashback to those days when women really were supposed to be in the home. But there is a wonderful interview with Irving Berlin, a Jew, about his song "White Christmas." Berlin recounts how when he was young his Christian neighbors invited him over for Christmas, and he in turn invited them over for Hanukah. Berlin claimed to be "delighted" that kids in school were learning to respect other faiths, but in the "old days we did this anyway."

While abortions were becoming more were available at Georgetown, Shakespeare was not. It had been dropped as a requirement for English majors.

On December 25, the *Post* reported on the Christmas happenings around town (eleven thousand had visited the Christmas pageant the day before), ran a photograph of a girl at her Christmas tree, and included a story about the pope — all on the front page. The lead editorial condemned increasing materialism and commercialism in Christmas and then concluded by claiming that Christianity is a superior theology and philosophy to what came before — and what comes after. The editors write, "There was love of a kind, no doubt, among men in the days of the Roman Saturnalia and the *libertas decembris* when masters changed places with their slaves; and there is some love, too, even in this tinseled, showy, materialistic world that surrounds us. But what this day should make us remember is that in human beings like ourselves love at its best is a reflection of God's great Christmas gift to this world, given long ago in Bethlehem, yet still given everywhere and at every instant to all who have the heart and will to desire it in an eternal Christmas."

Almost fifty years later, in 2003, the *Post*'s Christmas coverage wasn't nearly as ubiquitous. To be fair, it was not entirely lacking.

Stories about Christmas appear in the Metro, Food, and Style sections — although many are on the shopping, crafts, and preparation
aspects of the holiday. On the front page is a story ("Still Not Home
for the Holidays") on soldiers in Fallujah. Local news is good, including stories on a local choir and on how senior citizens celebrate
Christmas. The Christmas Day lead editorial is a hope for peace in
the Middle East, quoting Will Durant's book *Caesar and Christ*. On
the religion page is a lengthy — and good — story on an exhibit of
nativity scenes from around the world.

Yet while reading the 2003 Christmas coverage, I realized that the
amount of religion coverage the *Post* allocated for Christmas was the
amount of religion many American have in their lives not only at
the end of December, but every day. Many of us pray, read theology
books, and enjoy gospel music and choirs year round. We don't need
it to be Christmas to read historians like Will Durant and others interested in historical Christianity. We read magazines like *Christianity
Today*, *First Things* and, on the liberal side, *Sojourners*. We wouldn't
protest to see theologians, left and right, with weekly columns the
way Norman Vincent Peale appeared. In fact, we might even read
papers like the *Post* with more enthusiasm.

My essay "Prime Time Lent" ran on the front page of the Out-
look section, the part of the Sunday paper dedicated to politics and
culture. I didn't tell any of my family or friends that I had sold the
piece. I just wanted them to pick up the Sunday paper and read it.
At about eight in the morning, my dad called. He was thrilled, even
if he knew I wasn't much of a Catholic. Although my dad loved
the church, he never pushed us to remain Catholic. He was that
rare, pre-1960s combination of a political liberal — he believed in
the Vatican II declaration on the freedom of conscious and the importance of letting people decide what to believe for themselves —
and tough, orthodox Gonzaga Catholicism.

Despite my success with the *Post*, however, I soon realized it was
nearly impossible to make a career as a freelance writer, at least if
you weren't independently wealthy. I decided a smart track might be
through academia — getting a job at a university campus, where I
could take classes for free and be around intellectuals.

I got a job in the English department at Georgetown University. It seemed a perfect fit. I had gone to Georgetown Prep, and my grandfather had coached baseball at Georgetown. Dad was happy; if he hadn't received a scholarship to Catholic University, he would have gone to Georgetown. To him, the school was a monument to the toughness, the vitality of the faith — and the courage of John Carroll, the priest who founded the school in 1789.

It didn't take me long to figure out that Georgetown was no longer John Carroll's school. On my first week on the job a supervisor in the English department pulled me aside to explain something about the health benefits. The policy supposedly does not cover abortions, but she assured me that this was something of a joke. "There are easy ways around it," she said, waving her hand dismissively. (Is it any wonder that the student pro-abortion group runs editorials in the paper?) While abortions were becoming more available, Shakespeare was not. It had been dropped as a requirement for English majors. One professor taught using comic books.

In the Georgetown English department, one of the strangest professors — and that's saying a lot — was Father Ted Ingastetson, a young Jesuit priest. Ingastetson was obsessed with working out at the gym and was steeped in political correctness and deconstruction, the academic fad of the day. Ingastetson always acted hyperactive, as if he had just lifted weights and overdosed on vitamins and sea kelp. But he was not Father Herlihy, the macho priest from Gonzaga. Ingastetson was gay — very gay.

One of the courses he taught was called "Unspeakable Lives: Gay and Lesbian Narratives." That never bothered me, although the way he would breeze into the room and right to my desk, coming so close I thought I was about to be tackled, sometimes made me uneasy. He also never wore his clerical outfit — black shirt and white collar. He always had on wire-rimmed glasses, dress slacks, a shirt and tie, and expensive suspenders. He was more GQ than Vatican City.

Ingastetson's other love, besides working out and gay literature, was horror fiction — Stephen King, H. P. Lovecraft, and Clive Barker, among others. He taught a freshman course called "Horrors" that read horror fiction and then deconstructed it. I sat in on his class one day when he was teaching *American Psycho*, the pornographic slasher book by Brett Easton Ellis. "In what kind of culture does a text like this become possible?" he asked the class. "The book is a criticism of an idealized culture," one of the zombies regurgitated. "And what culture is that?" "The 1980s 'me' culture," the zombie replied. Ingastetson winced. "What is the first axiom of Father Ted's school of reading?" he asked.

No takers.

"Don't be seduced by point of view."

Another student tried to point out that the point of view was obvious — the name of the book is *American Psycho*.

"Never trust covers," Ingastetson rejoined. "They're like people — what you see is not what you get."

I had no idea what he was talking about. The student had succinctly summed up the point of *American Psycho*, but Ingastetson thought he was wrong. Apparently, as it turns out, everything in horror fiction boils down to fear of homosexuality.

Carrie, Salem's Lot, H. P. Lovecraft? Fear of gays.

American Psycho? Fear of gays.

Peanuts Halloween special? Fear of gays.

Ingastetson's class even made a *Washington Times* list of the dumbest, most PC courses in America. The night the paper came out, he returned to his dorm at Georgetown to find the article anonymously posted on the entrance bulletin board, with the line about him highlighted in yellow.

Ingastetson had been ordained in 1981, but wasn't long for the priesthood, which he left in the late 1990s. He told me when I was at Georgetown that he was not ordained "to be a rubber stamp," but apparently even the liberalism of Georgetown wasn't liberal enough. Ingastetson left Georgetown when he left the priesthood and joined a nondenominational Christian sect that pushes for gay marriage.

For all his faults, Ingastetson, if only through his "Horrors" course, did what few other professors did — talk about religion. The only other time I heard a reference to religion there was when the me-dieval scholars at the university put on a conference. It was some PC nonsense along the lines of "Queering the Middle Ages," and when I saw the flyer I laughed out loud. One of them heard me and asked me what the big joke was. I thought I was about to lose my job and tried to back away.

"I just don't get it," I sheepishly said. "Queering the Middle Ages? What the hell does that even mean?"

The professor smiled and patted me on the back.

"Oh, don't worry," he said. "We'll win you over to the devil's side."

As if I needed more proof that Georgetown was over the hump, one afternoon I came across a copy of *Georgetown at Two Hundred,* a book published in 1990. It was supposed to be a celebration of two centuries of Jesuit higher education on the Potomac, but some of it read more like a secular manifesto. Women's Studies profes-sor Leona Fisher contributed an essay, "The Challenge of Women's Studies: Questions for a Transformed Future at Georgetown." That transformed future, according to Fisher, required five admissions from the university:

1. That all courses not self-defined as "women's studies" or con-ceived to be feminist in methodology or women-centered in content are not "universal" but "men's studies."

2. That all courses not self-defined as "African American [or other] studies" or as racially or ethnically pluralistic are not "color-blind" but white-defined, ethnocentric, implicitly racist.

3. That all courses not naming themselves as concerned with class differences are implicitly biased toward the middle class.

4. That history is not a "given," but an almost infinitely redefin-able, revisable entity — and that we have a responsibility to redefine it over and over again in the interest of accuracy and honesty.

5. That all intellectual discourse and interpretations are "polit-ical" — that is, ideological and powerful — if only uncon-sciously. Those who would deny this do so because theirs is

the place of the secure insider in the discourse; their so-called "objectivity" is merely the subjectivity of the privileged group.

For a while, I could handle Georgetown's dumb, self-important radicalism. I just walked past the "safe zone" stickers on faculty doors, announcing to the world that that person's office was free from homophobia, sexism, racism — the usual chimeras. (A snippet of student-to-professor conversation I actually overheard one day: "I told my friends that it's actually easier being out at Georgetown than at home!") But ultimately, one event convinced me to leave.

I was walking down the hall and passed a group of three professors. "That's right," I overheard one say. "The revolution is going to start right here."

I waited for the laugh that was sure to follow such an idiotic statement. It never came. I decided that these people were delusional, suffering from the academic fever that rises when one is totally isolated from reality. Either that, or they were insane.

While many at Georgetown claimed, and still claim, that their hostility toward the church stemmed from a commitment to compassion and social justice, it was mostly about pure resentment. James Hitchcock summed this up nicely in his essay "The Root of American Violence." In it he claims that many calls for change in politics and the church are simple celebrations of the self. "What has happened," Hitchcock writes, has been

the abandonment of politics, or its annihilation, in favor of public and organized forms of therapy. Emphasis is less and less on the general material needs of the citizens, with which the state has some possibility of coping, and more and more on the formerly private, personal, and subjective aspect of lives, which the state is expected, somehow, to respond to in symbolically comforting ways. What the New Left primarily accomplished was to establish a particular style of public discourse which enables emotionally frustrated people to express themselves in cathartic ways.

Hitchcock notes that behind most church reformers is nothing more or less than plain resentment. The first modern philosopher to cite resentment as a broad cultural force was Friedrich Nietzsche. In *The Genealogy of Morals* and *The Birth of Tragedy*, Nietzsche claimed that *ressentiment* was the source of Christian morality. Christianity was in fact a "slave morality" that turned the natural order of things upside down: the losers in life were actually the winners, poverty was better than wealth. Nietzsche's assessment was off the mark, as noted by the German philosopher Max Scheler. Scheler, whose philosophy of phenomenology would be a major influence on the thinking of John Paul II, agreed with Nietzsche that resentment could be a social force, but insisted that Christian love in its genuine form was pure, selfless, and transforming.

I waited for the laugh that was sure to follow such an idiotic statement. It never came.

Scheler's ideas were examined and expanded by Hitchcock in an essay, "Guilt and the Moral Revolution." Hitchcock notes that the rise of resentment in the United States is a sign not of the weakness of the country, but its success. Resentment rises out of material wealth, the boredom of not having to worry about mere survival. Furthermore, the success of America's breakdown of social and class barriers has fueled resentment. Whereas Scheler thought that resentment would be most intense in societies with class distinctions like England and peter out in societies without such distinctions, the opposite is actually the case. As Hitchcock points out, "those societies which have gone far in the abolition of social distinctions merely invite more microscopic scrutiny of their structures." As an example, Hitchcock cites the New Left of the 1960s, which attacked liberals more ferociously than conservatives. Resentment, notes Hitchcock, is a modern disease caused by the supposed cure.

Yet Hitchcock's most important point is that, in the end:

Political and class distinctions are finally not at the heart of resentment. Morality is. It is the claim of some, whether implicit or explicit, conscious or unconscious, to represent an authoritative truth which inspires the bitterest hostility. It might even be argued that all social and political claims imply moral claims and that is why they are ultimately hated, with political or economic grievances put forth primarily as rationalizations for much deeper resentments.

Too many church reformers — not to mention the cultural elite — simply hate the idea of morality itself. They hate that certain moral codes are tightly logical and written on the human heart: no matter how much they fool with the language or talk around it, something will always tell them that abortion is wrong. (Hitchcock insightfully states that the pro-life movement should be glad when their arguments are met with vitriol on the other side; the fury explodes because the abortionists know what they are doing is wrong.)

Paradoxically, had my Catholic education resembled the "tyrannical" and medieval torture my father went through, I might well have been better adjusted. It was the very freedom that I enjoyed — or rather what I conceived to be freedom, which was nothing more than slavery to drugs and trends and self-destruction — coupled with the 1960s culture that insisted that reticence is unhealthy that made my hostility that much greater. Hitchcock: "Like all revolutions, [resentment] feeds on the weakness of the establishment, not its tyrannies. It is because the guardians of moral authority, especially the clergy but also parents, policemen, judges, and others, are visibly uncertain about their own beliefs, obviously willing to evade the responsibilities given to them, that resentment now appears so boldly." Hitchcock then sums up his thesis nicely:

> America in the 1970s produced a generation of materially comfortable, bored, self-obsessed individuals whose only conviction was to be "open" to all experiences. The inevitable effects of such a culture were asserted, over and over again, to be a spirit of peace, self-fulfillment, tolerance, and love. Instead the very possibility of love was destroyed, if love is thought to require

unselfish devotion to another. Rather the most common product of the "me decade" (not by any means only among the young) has been the aimless sensualist filled with resentment.

I quit my job at Georgetown, then wrote an article about my experience there, and sold it to the *Weekly Standard*, a politically conservative magazine that had just been launched. The faculty (so I heard) went nuts, going so far as to lie about me. A couple of months after I quit, I ran into a student I had become friends with. She told me she was "sorry about the lawyers." I had no idea what she was talking about. Apparently, to save face or just look tough, some faculty members had spread the word that they had marshaled lawyers to attack me, and I had been so intimidated that I had promised not to write anything else about the school. This was, and remains, pure fantasy.

If anything, Georgetown has gotten worse since I left. If the Marxist professors, the student Gay, Lesbian, Transgendered, and Questioning club, and the posters promoting pro-abortion rallies haven't shattered the illusion that Georgetown is Catholic, a 2004 issue of the *Hoya*, the student newspaper, will do so.

The issue was an April Fool's edition. Some of the gag articles and headlines are quite funny ("Angry Neighbors Invade Campus: French Department Promptly Surrenders"). On the inside is a parody of a rival paper, the *Georgetown Voice*. The lead editorial in the bogus *Voice*: "We're So F***Ing Cool." There are no asterisks in the actual parody — just as there is no doubt what is meant on the front page of the fake issue when the fax number for the paper is spelled to connote fornication.

There was no immediate faculty reaction to this, or rather, there was one letter sent to the paper by the Reverend Ryan Maher, a Jesuit. Father Maher's objection was, to put it generously, mild: "Mind you, I am a Jesuit: I am no stranger to off-color humor. I use it myself at the dinner table with my friends. I have applauded it on student stages when it has been used to artistic and dramatic effect. But prudence, judgment, and maturity tell even the slack-jawed that there's a time and a place for everything."

Of course, it would be foolish to expect anything else. This is the Father Maher who in January wrote a column in the *Hoya* about Father Edward Drinan, one of the most notorious Jesuits in American history — that is, if you consider a priest supporting abortion notorious. According to Maher, Drinan, "the man behind the legend," cared deeply for "human rights, the plight of refugees, migrant workers and the uninsured, and the environment." Drinan also publicly defended President Clinton's veto of the partial-birth abortion bill. He also supported Georgetown's pro-choice group, G. U. Choice. He was ultimately forced by the Vatican to recant these views, but no matter. To Maher, those who disagree that Drinan was the reincarnation of Dorothy Day are "un-Catholics" who "rail with the smug certitude of Pharisees." Gripe about a pro-abortion priest? What are we thinking? This is Georgetown.

No matter how much the folks in the recruitment office publish pictures of collared men in the brochures, there's just no way around it: not only is Georgetown no longer Catholic, it is hostile to the church and actively acts to subvert Catholic teaching. Student Brendan Faughnan, in a recent piece called "Where Have All the Catholics Gone?" in the *Georgetown Independent*, recounts that when he told a former Jesuit that he, Faughnan, regretted missing Mass so much, the man called him "a superstitious [expletive]." Faughnan noted that one Ash Wednesday less than half the student body had the cross marked on their foreheads.

Faughnan also reveals that the apparent victory in the crucifix controversy of a few years ago had been less than total. When many members of the faculty tried to ban the crucifix from new classrooms, they were forced to change by alumni and the few serious Catholic students still at the school. Many of the crosses, however, are from third world countries — a bow to political correctness — and have next to them signs explaining their stylistic origin. "While the signs may be interesting," Faughnan wrote, "I get the sneaking suspicion that the signs are there to lessen the presence of the crosses by treating them as if they were artifacts or pieces of art rather than a symbol of our faith."

– *Chapter Nine* –

Reversion

As mentioned before and as incredible as it may sound (or maybe not — does anything surprise us anymore?), a group of Catholic priests and scholars protested the new catechism even before its publication in 1994. In November 1989, a 434-page draft of the new catechism was sent out to three thousand of the world's bishops. A cover letter from Cardinal Ratzinger explained that the new catechism would be a "point of reference" and asked bishops for "observations, suggestions, and the proposals you deem opportune as to the entire draft of the catechism." This advanced preview was *sub secreto*, meaning that it was not to be released to third parties.

Apparently some theologians received bootleg copies of the catechism, because a little more than a month after its arrival a symposium was held, complete with fifteen scholarly papers, at the Woodstock Theological Center in Washington. Then on November 28, 1990, a meeting of a group called the Woodstock Forum was held at Georgetown University. The moderator was Father Thomas Rose, SJ, editor of the liberal Jesuit magazine *America*. The goal of the symposium was to celebrate the publication of the book *The Universal Catechism Reader*. *The Reader* consisted of the fifteen papers that had been presented at a January 1990 meeting at Georgetown.

At the November meeting, liberal Catholics asked rude questions whose sole purpose was to question the need for a new catechism.

"How could the pope and the bishops have been so stupid as to try to issue such a catechism?"

Another person demanded, "How can the thing be headed off?"

One theologian's answer was remarkable: "The catechism will be accepted in different ways. There will not be an open rejection of it, but if it is not helpful, it will be put on the shelf. Old church documents never die; they just gather dust. Just as in the case of *Humanae Vitae*, a teaching is not taught unless it is received." This was the cry of the catechetical obstructionists going back to Vatican II. Fortunately, the new catechism was published and became a giant bestseller.

My Catholic education began shortly after the catechism was published, with a priest named Richard John Neuhaus. Neuhaus is the editor of a magazine called *First Things*. In it he writes a monthly column, "The Public Square." In fact, it is really several columns in one, as it goes on for about twenty pages and involves observations that address various topics and range in length from a sentence to several pages.

I knew nothing about Neuhaus when I picked up a copy of *First Things* in the winter of 1995. The issue was actually for my father, who had left the *National Geographic* a few years earlier. Dad had worked at *National Geographic* for so long, no one in the family knew what he would do with himself. His period of adjustment lasted about an hour. Within a week he was laughing at the rush-hour traffic on the television, calling the commuters "suckers." He started going to Mass during the week and bird-watching early in the morning. He spent time at the race track, one of his favorite places when he was growing up. He also became fascinated with Demetrius Augustine Gallitzin, whom we discussed earlier in this book. Dad began taking day-trips to West Virginia to research Gallitzin's life. His desk became scattered with old Catholic manuscripts and books on Gallitzin, as well as maps of West Virginia, where Gallitzin had lived. Then Dad announced he was going to write a book about Gallitzin.

Dad spent a lot of his time reading and writing, and one night I noticed he had read, and corrected, a book about Catholicism I had been assigned at Catholic University.

The book was the work of a liberal theologian, and my dad had written his own comments — Wrong! or some variations on this — in the margins. Shortly after making this discovery I was in a bookstore and saw a copy of *First Things*. The names of the articles indicated it was a religious magazine and an intellectual one at that, and I thought Dad would enjoy it. I bought a copy.

Several weeks later I was looking for a book in my father's study when I saw the issue of *First Things* opened on his desk. He had it opened to "The Public Square," an installment about John Paul II's *Crossing the Threshold of Hope,* which had just been published. Neuhaus described how the book had been a huge bestseller even though the pope had had to cancel a trip to America. The press was baffled by this, but Neuhaus wasn't.

One night I noticed he had read, and corrected, a book about Catholicism I had been assigned at Catholic University.

"There is something funny going on here if we believe the prestige press, [which holds that] what we have in this book are disjointed philosophical and theological ramblings by a reflectionary old man who heads an authoritarian institution that is lamentably out of touch with most Catholics and the entirety of the modern world. Insight into what is going on here begins with not believing the prestige press." Neuhaus then quotes the pope: "We find ourselves faced with a new reality. The world tired of ideology is opening itself to the truth. The time has come when the splendor of the truth (*veritatis splendor*) has begun anew to illuminate the darkness of human existence." Neuhaus then emphasizes that John Paul II's hope was not to be confused with optimism, which is "merely a matter . . . of seeing what you want to see and not seeing what you don't want to see." To Neuhaus, "the hope in *Crossing the Threshold of Hope* is on the far side of a relentlessly realistic, indeed painfully bleak, understanding of human circumstance. Which is to say that it is on the far side of the Cross."

In all my years of Catholic education, I had never come across anything like this. Yet this didn't trigger a conversion. (Such instant turnovers are, in my view, rarely to be trusted anyway.) To tell the truth, I was as moved by the syntax, the quality of the prose, as I was by the message. I had been educated in the 1970s and 1980s. I didn't know that Catholics, aside from my father, knew how to write.

Yet there was also something in the message that pierced my heart. Neuhaus's phrase "the far side of the Cross" was a challenge to my ignorance — my belief, based on nothing, that Christianity was nothing but naive optimism and fairy tales. Either that, or this religion was the opposite: nothing but guilt fostered by constant exposure to the sight of a man being tortured. As Chesterton once noted, to critics Christianity can mean anything: it's at once too soft, too violent, a beautiful myth, and far too realistic and bloody. I was willing to call it all these things, but I was not willing to call it the truth.

Yet something small had changed with those six words — the far side of the Cross. Neuhaus was far too brilliant, his writing far too assured, his confidence too powerful, to dismiss out of hand.

That night, the incredible happened — I found myself defending Catholicism. It was a stumbling, blundering, foundering kind of a defense, but a defense nonetheless. I had a date with another journalist, and at some point the talk turned to Christianity. She began a tirade about the religious Right and how ignorant, dangerous, and downright dumb these Cro-Magnons were.

I started talking, and what came out of my mouth shocked me. I began to tell her about Neuhaus, about what he had written about the pope and realism on the far side of the Cross. She gave me that look that serious Christians get in public — like I had a dung beetle nailed to my forehead. The date ended shortly after.

Not long thereafter, in the winter of 1995, my father was diagnosed with cancer. He was sixty-eight and would live for only another six months. As I have said, Dad died with the dignity, soul, and humor with which he had lived. After my article about the radicalism at Georgetown was published in the *Weekly Standard*, I began writing regularly for that and other conservative magazines. One morning Dad, flat on his back in bed, read a piece I wrote celebrating Ronald Reagan. Dad finished the piece, blinked a couple times, and looked at me. "My last word is going to be 'amazing,'" he quipped. He could now barely get out of bed. Around his neck he wore a crucifix he had been given in Ireland.

Dad's death also showed the incredible strength left in the old Washington Catholic community. Calls came to the house every day from old classmates from Blessed Sacrament, Gonzaga, and Catholic University. My Prep buddies called and cleared their calendars to be there for the funeral. Old teachers of mine called, both from Prep and Mercy. Father Joseph Ranieri, one of Dad's oldest friends, arrived one afternoon to perform the last rites. Dad received his last Holy Communion, then Father Ranieri made the sign of the cross over Dad's head and spoke about my father's arriving departure. Standing around the bed was the family.

> *That night, the incredible happened. I found myself defending Catholicism. It was a stumbling, blundering, foundering kind of a defense, but a defense nonetheless.*

As the end was drawing near, Dad spilt a glass of water he was trying to drink. We had to change the sheets. I came to the side of the bed and drew him up in my arms, lifting him like a child — at that point he probably weighed eighty pounds. To the very last, he was giving himself to his family. Noticing the tears dropping off my chin, he tapped my shoulder to get my attention. "The thing that amazes me," he whispered, "is how easy dying is."

We told each other we loved each other. Shortly after, he was gone.

My father's funeral was held at Our Lady of Mercy, my old parish. My brother Michael delivered a brilliant eulogy. "The mystery of our sorrow, indeed the mystery of the universe itself, is now the province of the good man we have sent out on his last assignment." My father, Michael said, was his teacher. "He taught me the language that the trees speak at night when the wind blows just before dawn. He taught me to watch for the constellations that herald the seasons. He taught me to stand outside on Christmas Eve and smell the sharp, sacred air, and to wait with quiet joy through February's Lenten hush for the joy of Easter's spring, which dwelt in him through all seasons."

After my father's death, I entered a period of grief that is probably best and mostly simply described as black. As with my drinking, I feel no need to go into details — too much of that is not dignified, and my conversion, the subject at hand, had begun beforehand, with Neuhaus. Still, it was a difficult time for the entire family. Those who have gone through what the church calls a "dark night of the soul" know that the agony of grief and depression is often ineffable, residing in a place where human powers of description fail. The closest I've come to a genuine interpretation of such a place comes not from clinical journals or even poets but from some of the more unorthodox interpretations of Holy Saturday, the time between Jesus' crucifixion and his resurrection on Easter. What happens on Holy Saturday is one of the most stirring episodes in all of history. In the scriptures Christ descends into hell, or "the abode of the dead" — Sheol in the Hebrew and Hades in the Greek — to claim the souls of the righteous who came before him and to assume dominion over everything, both in heaven and hell. Some accounts in tradition even have Jesus coming for Adam, the first fallen man. The scene is set in one of my favorite sections of the *Catechism of the Catholic Church* (the source is given only as an "ancient homily for Holy Saturday"):

Today a great silence reigns on earth, a great silence and a great stillness. A great silence because the King is asleep. The earth trembled and is still because God has fallen asleep in the flesh and he has raised up all who have slept ever since the world began.... He has gone to search for Adam, our first father, as for a lost sheep. Greatly desiring to visit those who live in darkness and in the shadow of death, he has gone to free from sorrow Adam in his bonds and Eve, captive with him — He who is both their God and the son of Eve.... "I am your God, who for your sake have become your son.... I order you, O sleeper, to awake. I did not create you to be a prisoner in hell. Rise from the dead, for I am the life of the dead."

There are other interpretations of this event that are less triumphant. One of the more esoteric characters in Christian theology is Adrienne von Speyr, a Swiss mystic, author, and physician who died in 1967. Von Speyr had episodes where, beginning on Good Friday, she would go into a trance, become bedridden, and relive the passion of Jesus. As we saw, her mentor, a man who recorded some of these events, was Hans Urs von Balthasar, the brilliant twentieth-century Swiss priest and theologian. According to Von Speyr, Christ's descent to hell was somewhat different from the typical readings. In his book *First Glance at Adrienne von Speyr*, Balthasar explains:

> Hell is . . . the place where God is absent, where there is no longer the light of faith, hope, love, of participation in God's life; hell is what the judging God condemned and cast out of his creation; it is filled with all that is irreconcilable with God, from which he turns away for all eternity. It is filled with the reality of the world's godlessness, with the sum of the world's sin; therefore, with precisely all of that from which the Crucified had freed the world. In hell he encounters his own work of salvation, not in Easter triumph, but in the uttermost night of obedience, truly the "obedience of a corpse." He encounters the horror of sin separated from men. He "walks" through sin (without leaving a trace, since in hell and in death, there is neither time nor direction); and, transversing its formlessness, he experiences the second chaos. While bereft of any spiritual light emanating from the Father, in sheer obedience, he must seek the Father where he cannot find him under any circumstances.

I wish I could say that my reversion to Catholicism was triggered by some kind of explosive revelation, a bells-and-whistles event where I saw lights and heard angelic music. In fact, it was nothing like that. It was like falling in love with an old friend — and discovering that that love could always be begun anew.

It began, as I have described, with the discovery that the church had riches, intellectual riches, that I had hitherto not known about, having grown up at a time when many educators and leaders in the church had abandoned the best that had been thought and said in Catholicism. This included discovering Chesterton, Joseph Pieper, and other great thinkers of the church, among Dad's old books.

But faith, as the catechism explains, involves both the head and the heart. My head had reverted to Catholicism. My heart came second. It began when one afternoon I was at the Catholic U. library and decided to go into a building I had never set foot in while in college — the Basilica of the Shrine of the Immaculate Conception. Wandering through the quiet, endless expanse of the shrine I found myself literally surrounded by great Catholic figures I had never heard of before — with one exception. In the crypt church, the lower level of the shrine, there are walls and pillars etched with the names of faithful Catholics throughout history. One pillar near a statue of the Blessed Virgin Mary hails:

GALLITZIN

PRINCE PRIEST MISSIONARY

APOSTLE OF THE ALLEGHENIES

1840

It was my father's old friend, the Russian prince who became a priest and was the subject of the book Dad was working on when he died. Another friend of my dad's was represented in the shrine gift shop: they sell photographs of the shrine and the university taken by Fred Maroon, Dad's old friend from college and the other half of the "gold dust twins" who went to work for *Life* magazine after graduating.

Balthasar has written about the connection between beauty and the supernatural, and the shrine is a small city dedicated to beauty — the beauty of self-giving love exemplified by Christ, his mother, and the saints. The crypt church is a shimmering candlelit church modeled after the underground churches of early Christianity. It is ringed by apses on three sides, each apse featuring brilliant pictures of different saints: saints whose names and deeds are a mystery to most Catholic kids. There is St. Brigid of Ireland, born around A.D. 450. She is the patroness of babies, blacksmiths, and midwives. Next to her is St. Margaret of Antioch, who was disowned by her father when she converted to Christianity. A Latin inscription next to her reads, "Send forth your light and your truth that they may lead and guide me to your holy mountain and into your holy dwelling."

Many of the saints were martyrs who died in horrible ways. St. Agatha of Sicily turned away a suitor, Quintianus, who had her tortured. She had her breasts cut off and was then beheaded. St. Lucy, a fourth-century virgin and martyr, had her eyes plucked out before being put to death. St. Agnes was thirteen when she was martyred. The story goes that she had given her life to Christ and turned down the governor's son when he proposed marriage. As a result she was dragged through the streets to a brothel. Legend has it that she was saved from the brothel by an angel but was later decapitated.

Off the foyer outside the crypt church is a small chapel with a replica of the grotto where the Blessed Virgin appeared at Lourdes, and it was here that the conversion of my heart began. Again, I wish it involved lightning and thunder and epiphanies, but that would be a lie. What happened was fairly simply: I knelt down in the Lourdes chapel and talked to the Virgin Mary.

I had never done that before. Sure, there had been Hail Marys at Our Lady of Mercy and Georgetown Prep, and perhaps a plea to stop the room from spinning those times when I had too much to drink, but I could not recall a single time I had simply spoken to the Blessed Mother in a conversational tone and from the heart. But perhaps I was tired that day from walking around the shrine and just didn't feel like saying prayers from memory — prayers that I wasn't even sure meant anything.

So I knelt there and spoke to my Mother. I didn't try to inflate my language to fit the occasion. I just told her about my father's death, about Chesterton, about how beautiful I thought her shrine was. Then I asked her to let me do what God wanted me to do with my life. It was that simple.

That's when I started to feel it: peace of soul. Not a peace that lasted more than a few minutes, not a peace that gave me a beatific vision of heaven, not a peace that led to the Christian triumphalism and feel-good cocksureness of the TV preacher. It was just the feeling, for a few minutes, that when I was near the Blessed Mother I was near my true home. It was a brief but deep feeling, and one that had come to me simply because I had done nothing more complicated than go to it.

It always amazes me that people who criticize the Catholic Church do not give it the same chance that they give a new brand of toothpaste. Most are unwilling to simply sit in a church and talk to God for five minutes. They might find something that all the pills, drinks, and sex haven't been able to provide. They might find peace. Of course, it is peace with a foot planted in reality, that is, peace coupled with the willingness to accept our humanity in full, both our existence as holy creations of God and as prideful sinners who think we can make up our own value system and decide, based on our own conscience, what is right and wrong.

Along with the feeling of peace came feelings of fear. This may seem a strange sensation to have in a church, but it's really not. The great Franciscan friar Benedict Groeschel has written about the sense of fear that comes with contemplative prayer. He explains that it stems from the idea that God may actually ask us to do what he asks us to do in the New Testament — take up our cross and follow him. Indeed, part of the struggle of becoming serious about the faith is that it will reveal exactly what God wants from us.

So my Catholic reversion wasn't a thunderbolt as much as a slow immersion into reality — the reality of the spiritual realm, whose depth is beyond measure. I often compare it to slipping off a boat into the clear waters of an unfathomable sea. The bottom appears to be just below the surface, but in fact it is hundreds of feet down or more. And every time you think you're getting to the bottom, it expands to greater depths. This gentle way of experiencing the mystery of Christ is probably for the best; if God revealed too much of himself it would be difficult to take. On the feast of St. Nicolas in 1273 St. Thomas Aquinas returned from Holy Mass, but he was not the same man. The genius of the church and author of the massive *Summa Theologica* had no interest in finishing the work. He had had a vision, something so incredible it could not be described. His friend Reginald asked Thomas several times why he could not write and could barely speak. Finally St. Thomas answered: "All that I have written seems to me nothing but straw ... compared to what I have seen and what has been revealed to me." He died shortly after.

When I left the Lourdes chapel, I decided to do something I hadn't done in years — go to confession, which was offered in another chapel in the shrine. I also decided that I wasn't going to itemize all my sins over the past years, but, as with my conversation with the Blessed Mother, take it slow and easy, just one small step at a time. I was going to talk about something that had always bothered me: premarital sex, and Christ's teaching that anyone who has committed adultery in his heart has committed the sin itself. For years I found this impossible to square. As a healthy heterosexual male, how could I not want to be with a woman, much less walk down the street without admiring an attractive female? It was wired into my evolution and DNA.

It always amazes me that people who criticize the Catholic Church do not give it the same chance that they give a new brand of toothpaste.

I entered the confessional, which was different from the dark cubbyholes I remembered from my youth. There was a small table and lamp, and room enough for two chairs facing each other as well as a kneeler behind a curtain to the side. I could kneel sight unseen or face the priest. I decided to face the priest.

The priest was a hundred years old if he was a day. He had a long bushy white beard and was so skinny his legs looked like sticks under his monastic robe. I was disappointed. How could I talk about lust to this guy? Yet something inside me told me to go ahead with it. That was the sin I was worried about, so it was the one I should talk about. I made the sign of the cross and began the words I remembered from childhood: "Bless me Father, for I have sinned. It's been years since my last confession."

"Speak up," he said.

I looked at him. He was cupping a hand to his ear. He looked like a Civil War veteran who had shellshock.

I almost laughed. Here I was in confession for the first time in years, there were people waiting outside for their turn, and I was going to have to shout my sins of lust for the whole world to hear. I spoke louder, and he began to nod. I explained a little bit about who I was, mentioned my drinking, then zeroed in on the topic: How can you leave the house and not look at women?

He folded his hands gently. "Oh, it's okay to look," he said. "But maybe you should look at them the way Joseph looked at Mary."

I blinked. What?

"Joseph looked at Mary as a gift from God," he said, "and that's what women are — a holy and sacred gift from God."

I suddenly remembered that in second grade I had played Joseph in the Christmas play at Our Lady of Mercy.

This was an example of how the simple wisdom of Catholicism can alter perceptions, bringing them in closer line with reality. This servant of God wasn't telling me to shun the sexual urge as much as to accept it as part of my nature and put it in the service of something higher. He wasn't demanding I flee from reality; he was asking me to see reality — to acknowledge the miracle that was in front of my face.

This notion of seeing what is in front of you is central to Catholicism. In his wonderful book *Letters to a Young Catholic*, George Weigel explores how Catholicism embraces both the visible world and supernatural world and sees and lives the connection between the two. Weigel takes the reader on a tour of Catholic sights: Baltimore in the 1950s, the time and place of Weigel's youth; Chartres Cathedral in France; Castle Howard in Yorkshire, where they filmed Evelyn Waugh's *Brideshead Revisited*; the Basilica of the Holy Trinity in Krakow, Poland; even the Olde Chesire Cheese, the pub in England that was the playground of G. K. Chesterton.

Along the way, Weigel explains that Catholicism, as a sacramental faith, has a "grittiness" to it, a here-and-now quality that embraces the world, albeit the fallen world, even while it believes in things unseen. In effect, writes Weigel, Catholics have one foot in the visible and one in the invisible. He calls it the Catholic both/and: "nature and grace, faith and works, Jerusalem and Athens, faith and reason, charismatic and institutional, visible and invisible." Ironically, it is this duality that leads to what Weigel sees as a fierce realism:

> This distinctive Catholic worldliness is ever more important in a world that, by taking itself with ultimate seriousness, doesn't take itself seriously enough. Taking the world seriously doesn't mean falling into the trap of materialism and skepticism. Taking the world seriously means taking the world for what it is — the arena of God's action, the place where we meet the love that satisfies our yearning for a love that satisfies absolutely and without reservation.

Weigel rejects what he calls "Catholic Lite," that is, a modern Catholicism that is really no different from liberal Protestantism. In the chapter where Weigel visits the Oratory in Birmingham, England, where Cardinal John Henry Newman lived, he ties Newman's rejection of "liberal religion" to the current enthusiasm for gnosticism — the idea that the goal of religion is to separate one from the world and that the divine can be found within. Weigel nicely inverts the New Age cliché that life is a journey: "Newman's life and work remind us that the quest for truth is one of the greatest of human quests — if we understand that the purpose of the journey is not the journey itself but getting to the destination which is the light."

Believing in that light is not, as I once thought, a restrictive and authoritarian way of thinking, but a key to freedom. As St. Augustine noted, to be truly free we must first be free from certain things: lust, greed, murder, envy. What modern Catholics, especially those in the teaching professions, often fail to emphasize is that in letting these things go we can enter a world that is every bit as real, and thereby experience the kind of love that had driven us to indulge in those vices in the first place.

Of course, to be truly free we must accept God's law. Without this, we are left to ourselves, like drivers without traffic lights. Left to ourselves we make up our own rules, which ends up in addiction, violence, totalitarianism, and other disasters. Unlimited freedom paradoxically destroys our freedom. Pope John Paul II brilliantly

explores this in his masterpiece, the 1993 encyclical *Veritatis Splendor*
(The Splendor of Truth):

Rational reflection and daily experience demonstrate the weakness which marks man's freedom. That freedom is real but
limited: its absolute and unconditional origin is not in itself,
but in the life within which it is situated and which represents for it, at one and the same time, both a limitation and
a possibility. Human freedom belongs to us as creatures; it is
a freedom which is given as a gift, one to be received like a
seed and to be cultivated responsibly. It is an essential part of
that creaturely image which is the basis of the dignity of the
person. Within that freedom there is an echo of the primordial
vocation whereby the Creator calls man to the true Good, and
even more, through Christ's revelation, to become his friend
and to share in his own divine life. It is at once inalienable
self-possession and openness to all that exists, in passing beyond self to knowledge and love of the other. Freedom then
is rooted in the truth about man, and is ultimately directed
toward communion.

Reason and experience not only confirm the weakness of
human freedom, they also confirm its tragic aspects. Man comes
to realize that his freedom is in some mysterious way inclined to
betray this openness to the True and the Good, and that all too
often he actually prefers to choose finite, limited and ephemeral
goods. What is more, within his errors and negative decisions,
man glimpses the source of a deep rebellion, which leads him
to reject the Truth and the Good in order to set himself up
as an absolute principle unto himself: "You will be like God"
(Gen. 3:5). Consequently, freedom itself needs to be set free. It
is Christ who sets it free: he "has set us free for freedom."

Christ reveals, first and foremost, that the frank and open
acceptance of truth is the condition for authentic freedom: "You
will know the truth, and the truth will set you free" (John 8:32).
This is truth which sets one free in the face of worldly power
and which gives strength to endure martyrdom. So it was with

Jesus before Pilate: "for this I was born, and for this I have come into the world, to bear witness to the truth" (John 18:37). The true worshippers of God must thus worship him "in spirit and truth" (John 4:23): in this worship they become free. Worship of God and relationship with truth are revealed in Jesus Christ as the deepest foundation of freedom.

Furthermore, Jesus reveals by his whole life, and not only by his words, that freedom is acquired in love, that is, in the gift of self. The one who says: "Greater love has no man than this, that a man lay down his life for his friends" (John 15:13), freely goes out to meet his Passion (cf. Matt. 26:46), and in obedience to the Father gives his life on the Cross for all men (cf. Phil. 2:6–11). Contemplation of Jesus Christ Crucified is thus the highroad which the Church must tread every day if she wishes to understand the full meaning of freedom: the gift of self in service to God and one's brethren. Communion with the Crucified and Risen Lord is the never-ending source from which the Church draws unceasingly in order to live in freedom, to give oneself and to serve. Commenting on the verse in Psalm 100, "Serve the Lord with gladness," Saint Augustine says: "In the house of the Lord, slavery is free. It is free because it serves not out of necessity, but out of charity. . . . Charity should make you a servant, just as truth has made you free. . . . You are at once both a servant and free: a servant, because you have become such; free, because you are loved by God your creator; indeed, you have also been enabled to love your Creator. . . . You are a servant of the Lord and you are a freedman of the Lord. Do not go looking for a liberation which will lead you far from the house of your liberator!"

— *Chapter Ten* —

The Passion

In the winter of 2003, I attended my twentieth reunion at George-town Prep. All my old buddies were there, and when we congregated in the old dining room they gave out old copies of the *Unknown Hoya* and showed our cinematic masterpiece *Derelict Death Wish*, which, twenty years after its premier, still brought down the house.

Talking to them, their parents, and my old teachers, I discovered that there was good and bad news from Prep. In many ways the school seemed to have started shaking off its 1960s hangover. There was a new statue of Ignatius Loyola in the quad. There was a new emphasis on helping the poor and disabled. Students often traveled to third world countries to build houses and install water pumps, and there was a new baseball camp for the physically and developmentally disabled.

Yet in other ways Prep was either the same or far worse. A recent issue of *Alumnews*, a magazine put out by Prep, published a survey of alumni. Asked what the most valuable aspect of "the Prep experience" was, the answers were these:

1. friends
2. preparation for college
3. preparation for life

Asked what the school's current mission should be, the answers were these:

1. preparing students for life
2. preparing students for college
3. imparting spiritual values

The top reason for giving to the school was to "continue the academic quality." Note how being prepared for life and imparting spiritual values are considered totally separate things. It's hard to imagine a public school that couldn't have come up with identical answers.

The curriculum at Prep had barely changed since I had been there. I asked one of my old teachers how any of the kids could graduate without knowing who G. K. Chesterton was, and he just gave me a blank look. Didn't he know what Chesterton had done for a previous generation of moderns in a secular world? When it was first published in 1908, journalist Wilfred Ward declared that *Orthodoxy* was "the administration of intellectual stimulants, or the application to a tired and bored world of a tremendous shower-bath in order to brace it and renew its normal activities.... The spectacle of this intensely active and earnest modern intellect...reminds us how much that is indispensable in the inheritance of Christendom our own age has ceased adequately to understand and is in danger of lightly abandoning." The writer Dorothy L. Sayers credited *Orthodoxy* with helping her remain a Christian. At the time the book was published, she was a schoolgirl who had grown tired of her Anglican Christianity. Then she read *Orthodoxy.* In 1952 she recalled the experience: "To the young people of my generation, G. K. Chesterton was a kind of Christian liberator. Like a beneficent bomb, he blew out of the Church a quantity of stained glass of a very poor period, and let in gusts of fresh air in which the dead leaves of doctrine danced with all the energy and indecorum of Our Lady's tumbler."

I tried to explain to my old teacher that Chesterton, like Neuhaus, Merton, and John Paul II, is not offering the world an escape from reality in the form of a childish fantasy, but a bold leap into the heart of reality. As Fulton Sheen put it, Christ didn't run from the world; he entered it and drank death like water. Man is naturally a mystic and performed rituals before he could speak, Chesterton insisted. In fact, the people who are absolutely rational and logical to the exclusion of the mystical and supernatural are those who are in insane asylums. "The madman's explanation of a thing is always complete, and often in a purely rational sense satisfactory.... If a man says (for instance) that men have a conspiracy against him, you cannot dispute it except by saying that all the men deny that they are conspirators; which is exactly what conspirators would do. His explanation covers the facts as much as yours." The mind of the lunatic "moves in a perfect but narrow circle."

On the other hand, Christianity allows the mystery that human nature recognizes as part of the order of things. "The Christian permits free will to remain a sacred mystery.... He puts the seed of dogma in a central darkness; but it branches forth in all directions with abounding natural health." While the circle represents logic that refuses religion and the supernatural and thus leads to insanity, the Cross signifies freedom. "For the circle is perfect and infinite in its nature; but it is fixed forever in its size; it can never be larger or smaller. But the Cross, though it has at its heart a collision and a contradiction, can extend its four arms forever without altering its shape. Because it has a paradox in its center it can grow without changing. The circle returns upon itself and is bound. The cross opens its arms to the four winds; it is a signpost for free travelers." Free travelers like my dad.

Yet even if Prep and other Catholic schools began assigning Catholic reading, the message of such writing can even be subverted in the very pages of the book in question. I recently bought a new edition of *The Seven Storey Mountain*, Thomas Merton's autobiography and one of my dad's favorite books. I was surprised to discover that extras were added to the book in 1998 — an introduction by Robert Giroux and "A Note to the Reader" by William H. Shannon, the president of the International Thomas Merton Society. Giroux's introduction is a fine one, a short reflection on Merton and the story of how the book became a surprise bestseller. Shannon's piece, not to put too fine a point on it, is an offensive, smug, anti-Catholic disaster. It is not too much to call it a calumny and defacement. "The Roman Catholic Church you encounter in this book," Shannon pronounces, "is almost light years removed from the church that we recognize as the Roman Catholic Church today. Today's church is the product of the revolution (not too strong a term) set in motion by the Second Vatican Council." Shannon doesn't pull any punches:

The pre–Vatican II church into which Merton was baptized was a church still reacting — even three centuries later — to the Protestant Reformation of the sixteenth century. Characterized by a siege mentality, wagons circled around doctrinal and moral absolutes, it clung to its past with great tenacity. An institution apart, it showed little desire to open itself to the questions and needs of a world undergoing huge and unprecedented changes. The church prided itself on the stability and unchangeable character of its teaching in the context of a world in flux. At the time Merton wrote his book, Roman Catholic theology had become a set of prepackaged responses to any and all questions. Polemical and apologetic in tone, its aim was to prove Catholics were right and all others were wrong.

So the Catholic Church had the stunning gall to claim it stood for moral absolutes. Unlike those open-minded Protestant denominations? Worse, it insisted that it provided timeless answers — or wisdom "ever ancient and ever new," in Augustine's phrase — that transcended the fads of the day. Further, it claimed that it had the truth and other sects and denominations — gasp — did not. Such malevolence was obviously behind Merton's next unforgivable sin: the "complacent triumphalism" that leads him to think he belongs to the "one true" church (note the scare quotes around that phrase). This triumphalism also causes him to disparage other Christian denominations. This is simply beyond the pale, Shannon suggests, but modern, enlightened readers will simply have to hold their noses: "Readers today will be better able to put this narrowness in historical perspective and thus be less bothered by it."

The Seven Storey Mountain is a deeply moving, beautiful, funny, and spiritually stirring autobiography of a man who left the world for the riches of a life in God. It is also a book written by a man who fell deeply in love with the Catholic Church and made no apologies for it. It is not a liberal, secular book — although, like almost every Catholic teacher I ever had, Shannon tries to drag the church into the modern age rather than have the modern age move to the church. In his note Shannon offers this summation:

People continue to read *The Seven Storey Mountain* because the story of how Merton arrives at this certitude is so compelling. We are swept along with this young man as he seeks to make something out of his heretofore undisciplined life. Today, as we hover on the verge of a new millennium, we can identify with his searching, if not always with the specific direction it took. Merton's personal magnetism, the enthusiasm of his convictions, the vivid narratives of this born writer, transcend the narrowness of his theology. His story contains perennial elements of our common human experience. This is what makes it profoundly universal.

So: *The Seven Storey Mountain* is not a Catholic book. It is a New Age tale of self-discovery, easily adaptable to the culture of Oprah. It's all about the imperial self and the search for, well, me. Forget the direction Merton's search took. In fact, forget the point of the entire book. Pay no attention to Merton's rhapsodies about Mary, Jesus, the saints, and the church that gave him his salvation and the salvation of the world. Don't even bother with the Latin. It's all part of that narrow theology. Chesterton once remarked that he loved the Catholic Church because it had prevented him from becoming a child of his age. William Shannon, sadly, is very much a child of his age. I dare say that in a hundred years his introduction to Merton's masterpiece will seem far more dated than the text it introduces. Indeed, it is Merton who gets the last word on Shannon, not the other way around. It occurs when Merton realizes the error of his old life:

> I saw clearly enough that I was the product of my times, my society, and my class. I was something that had been spawned by the selfishness and irresponsibility of the materialistic century in which I lived. However, what I did not see was that my own age and class only had an accidental part to play in this. They gave my egoism and pride and my other sins a peculiar character of weak and supercilious flippancy proper to this particularly century: but that was only on the surface. Underneath, it was the same old story of greed and lust and self-love, of the three

concupiscences bred in the rich, rotted undergrowth of what is technically called "the world," in every age, in every class.

To be fair, there are still some great teachers in Catholic schools — and with young people increasingly turning to orthodoxy, an increasing possibility of a rediscovery of the true wisdom and reality of the church. Indeed, my experience there was far from a total loss. As I was digging through my father's old books and papers after he died, I came across a letter that had been written to me in 1986 by Father Hart, the beloved teacher at Prep I mentioned earlier, who loved rock and roll and C. S. Lewis and called my class "brewheads." (Father Hart died as I was finishing the writing of this book. It was a great loss to me and to many others.) It was Father Hart who first encouraged me to read Dante, and the good father exchanged letters with me for years after I graduated from Prep.

So: The Seven Storey Mountain *is not a Catholic book. It is a New Age tale of self-discovery, easily adaptable to the culture of Oprah.*

I had sent him a tape with rock songs on it, including "King of Pain," a song by the Police, my favorite band at the time. I hoped to convey to him that the truth wasn't in the Bible or the Mass, but in the truth of the pain expressed in great rock songs — life sucks, it's full of misery, there is no God, and the only true expression of humanity is rebellion. It was pure narcissism. I included a letter in which I, the wise atheist, sarcastically asked him, a priest, if he was "still going to mass." I also mentioned that I had seen *Gandhi*, a film he recommended, and that I enjoyed it. Father Hart's reply is one that speaks to me — and the entire rock-and-roll generation. His reference to "the Ring" is the evil ring from *The Lord of the Rings* — the ring that turns the healthy into an evil, greedy shadow of themselves:

I watched the Synchronicity concert on HBO the other night. I'm sorry to have to tell you that I was disappointed in Sting, though I thought the other two guys in the band were outstanding. I am afraid that your hero was a bit burnt out, perhaps from the bizarre lifestyle the superstars can get into, especially when they are touring. Sting looked bloated and acted sloppy. It seemed to me that for the most part he was not interested enough in his songs to try and do them with all his attention. I wonder if Sting hasn't been slipping on the Ring lately — and you know what happens to those who try to use the Ring.

Just before sitting down to write you I listened to a few of the numbers from the tape you made — songs like Don McLean's "Crossroads" and George Harrison's "Beware of Darkness" — and they sent me on a train of thought — about pain. It just so happens that one of the songs Sting did relatively well was "King of Pain." Even though he's been overdoing the painkillers of all types, I think it's a subject he can be serious about. . . .

Then there's the piece by Don McLean: "Can you find my pain? Can you heal it?" What is this pain they are talking about, Mark? Do you know? I know a little bit about my own, and I know that everyone has it — but I know that each person's pain is as personal as their name. And I know that it's worse to try and cover it and hide from it than accept it.

I was very happy that you saw the movie *Gandhi*, and even happier that you were impressed by it. Gandhi could live as he did because way down deep he had accepted the pain without protest. And he could do that because he also found a Life strong enough to absorb the pain without needing to resist — and being able to live that way is what I call salvation. In case you're wondering, I am driving at something. It's the Eucharist. I was fascinated that you asked me if I was still going to mass — and because of that I can't help mentioning it in connection with these other things.

How do you think Gandhi could ever walk around the way he did and see people as he saw them and treat them as he did? For myself I am sure it was not simply because he was a very strong individual with great moral character. I am sure that it was because he was in contact with God. Like Jesus, it wasn't just at his death that he offered the sacrifice of his life. That is the way he lived, and that is the very life we as Catholics are called to live — not necessarily in the heroic scale of Gandhi, but in the way we treat ordinary people. To live that way is to offer a sacrifice to God — it is what the mass calls being a "living sacrifice of praise." The very action of living and dying that way is what is celebrated in the Eucharist — and if you know that and look quietly and with respect into the celebration itself, you may find there a source of strength more surprising than anything else you've experienced. My experience is that it grows on you gradually. If you accuse me of preaching I can answer that you asked for it by wondering out loud if I was going to mass.

A few more Father Harts, and Catholic education may survive. It also wouldn't hurt if a movement was started to make sure every Catholic kid read at least ten classic books by the time he graduated from high school. By now you can guess what's on my list: Chesterton's *Orthodoxy*, Merton's *The Seven Storey Mountain*, *Letters to a Young Catholic* by George Weigel, *The Intellectual Life* by Sertillanges, *Death on a Friday Afternoon* by Richard Neuhaus, *Transformation in Christ* by Dietrich von Hildebrand, *The Four Cardinal Virtues* by Josef Pieper, *The Confessions of St. Augustine*, *Life of Christ*, by Fulton J. Sheen, and *Four Witnesses*, by Rod Bennett, which recounts the life of the early church.

It also may be time for Catholics to take a lesson from old Father "Nails" Herlihy, the terror of Gonzaga, and learn how to, well, hate again. Not to hate people but to hate evil, to hate stupidity, and to hate ignorance — especially ignorance of our own faith. Probably the best primer on virtuous hate I ever read was in a long-forgotten little pamphlet that came out in 1972. It's called *A Priest for All Seasons: Masculine and Celibate,* and was written by Conrad W. Baars, a Christian psychiatrist who was a consultant to the Vatican. Much of the problem in the priesthood, Baars noted, is the lack of masculinity — a masculinity intertwined with a healthy hatred of evil. His ideas, he acknowledged, will sound "strange in times in which so many wish for love and fulfillment, and equate charity with not hurting other people's feelings. Strange in times that too many priests, in seeking to promote peace and justice, seem . . . meek in the defense of absolute truths." He goes on:

> The idea of modern man — and a priest at that — being a fighter may seem ridiculous when those to whom the welfare of society has been entrusted imagine, as Josef Pieper says, the power of evil not so gravely dangerous that one could not "negotiate" or "come to terms with it." It seems that personal charity, brotherly love, and fortitude need to play only a subordinate role in a welfare society whose liberalistic world view — characterized by a resolute worldliness, an earthy optimism, and a middle-class metaphysics, anxiously bent on security — is blind to the existence of evil in the world of men, as well as in the world of spirits.

The idea that evil exists and deserves our fear and loathing was resurrected a few weeks after the Prep reunion, when Mel Gibson released his film *The Passion of the Christ*. Gibson's film displayed how the deep Catholic belief in the supernatural imbues us with a more vivid imagination than other religions — and even other Christian denominations. It's hard to imagine *The Passion* being made by a non-Catholic — even a Christian non-Catholic. Chicago priest and author Andrew Greeley, in his 2000 book *The Catholic Imagination*, explains that more than any other faith, Catholicism sees the world as enchanted. Through the sacraments ordinary objects — bread, wine, the human body — become manifestations of God's grace. This is a contrast to other religions, which tend to reject creation as an impediment to enlightenment (Buddhism) or as something comparable to a roach farm compared to the glory of God (Islam and fundamentalist Christianity).

For Catholics, the world can explode with manifestations of God. The supernatural can be felt not just in prayer, but in everything from the beach at night to rock and roll to modern art. Indeed, the great Catholic philosopher Etienne Gilson defended modern art in Catholic terms. In his 1955 book *Painting and Reality*, Gilson writes:

"Reduced to its simplest expression, the function of modern art has been to restore painting to its primitive and true function, which is to continue through man the great creative activities of nature. In so doing, modern painting has destroyed nothing and condemned nothing that belongs in any one of the legitimate activities of man; it has simply regained the clear awareness of its own nature and recovered its own place among the creative activities of man."

Not to hate people but to hate evil, to hate stupidity, and to hate ignorance — especially ignorance of our own faith.

Even with Mel Gibson's help, it may be an uphill climb to restore the healthy hate Baars talks about, and the sense of the supernatural that my dad's generation took for granted, especially with the media and fellow Catholics working against it. There are also the temptations of material wealth and entitlement, which have corrupted too many Catholic schools. At the reunion one of the administrators at Prep told me that the kids at the school had a sense of entitlement comparable to Hollywood celebrities. To too many of the status-obsessed parents, the kids are going to have the best in life, period, and the kids can do no wrong.

In a brilliant speech in 2003, theologian David B. Hart explained how the most tragic thing about the modern age is that all gods have been abandoned with the exception of the god of the will. Hart noted that early Christians had a ritual during baptism that revealed the chasm between the pagan and the Christian worlds. The adult convert, before wading into the baptismal pool, would turn to the west and reject the devil and the devil's ministers — as Hart put it, reviling "the gods in bondage to whom he had languished all his life." Turning to the east he confessed his devotion to Christ, or "entrusting himself to the invincible hero who had plundered hell of its captives, overthrown death, subdued the powers of the air, and been raised the Lord of History."

Most people in the modern world, including Catholics, lack even the grim resignation to fate that belonged to those who cowered from the Fates and the Furies; today people follow the god of the will. This leads to despair and the worship of nothingness. Hart:

> Modern persons will never find rest for their restless hearts without Christ, for modern culture is nothing but the wasteland from which the gods have departed, and so this restlessness has become its own deity; and deprived of the shelter of the sacred and the conjoining myths of sacrifice, the modern person must wander or drift, vainly attempting one or another accommodation with death, never escaping anxiety or ennui, and driven as a result to a ceaseless labor of distraction, or acquisition, or willful idiocy. And, where it works its sublimest magic, our culture of empty spectacle can so stupefy the intellect as to blind it to its own disquiet, and induce a spiritual torpor more deplorable than mere despair.

The answer to this spiritual torpor is the Risen One, Christ, the Harrower of Hell whom we meet in the heart of joy and suffering. He is the One who took our spiritual despair, experienced it on the cross, and through love transformed it into love. It would be nice to reintroduce him and those who worship him — Aquinas, Augustine, St. Teresa, Chesterton, von Hildebrand, Neuhaus — into the curriculum of Catholic schools, which are still in bad shape. According to a recent report, at many major Catholic universities students are leaving less Catholic than they were when they entered. We can only hope that some of them have Catholic parents who keep old Catholic books in the basement.

Works Cited

Asci, Donald P. *The Conjugal Act as a Personal Act: A Study of the Catholic Concept of the Conjugal Act in the Light of Christian Anthropology.* San Francisco: Ignatius Press, 2002.

Augustine. *The Confessions of St. Augustine.* Translated, with an introduction and notes, by John K. Ryan. New York: Doubleday, 1960.

Baars, Conrad W. *A Priest for All Seasons: Masculine and Celibate.* Chicago: Franciscan Press, 1972.

Balthasar, Hans Urs von. *First Glance at Adrienne von Speyr.* Translated by Antje Lawry and Sr. Sergia Englund. San Francisco: Ignatius Press, 1981.

Baum, Gregory. *New Horizon: Theological Essays.* New York: Paulist, 1972.

Bennett, Rod. *Four Witnesses: The Early Church in Her Own Words.* San Francisco: Ignatius Press, 2002.

Braaten, Carl E. "Toward a Theology of Hope." *Theology Today* 24, no. 2 (July 1967): 208–26.

Buchanan, Patrick J. *Right from the Beginning.* Boston: Little, Brown, 1988.

———, ed. *God, Jesus, and Spirit.* New York: Herder & Herder, 1969.

Catechism of the Catholic Church. 2nd ed. Vatican City: Libreria Editrice Vaticana, 2000.

Chesterton, G. K. *The Man Who Was Thursday: A Nightmare.* New York: Capricorn Books, 1960.

———. *Orthodoxy.* San Francisco: Ignatius Press, 1995.

Church, The. "Under the Milky Way." *Under the Milky Way: The Best of the Church.* Original recording remastered, 1999. Buddha/Bmg audio CD 99652.

Conquest, Robert. *Reflections on a Ravaged Century.* New York: Norton, 2000.

Cook, Bernard J. *The God of Space and Time.* New York: Holt, Rinehart & Winston, 1969.

Cunningham, Lawrence S. *Francis of Assisi: Performing the Gospel Life.* Grand Rapids, Mich.: W. B. Eerdmans, 2004.

Curran, Charles. *Christian Morality Today: The Renewal of Moral Theology.* Notre Dame, Ind.: Fides Publishing, 1966.

Denizet-Lewis, Benoit. "Whatever Happened to Teen Romance?" *New York Times Magazine,* May 30, 2004.

Dulles, Avery, SJ. *The Reshaping of Catholicism: Current Challenges in the Theology of Church.* San Francisco: Harper & Row, 1988.

Durant, Will and Ariel. *Caesar and Christ.* Vol. 3, *The Story of Civilization.* New York: Simon & Schuster, 1944.

Fisher, Lorna. "The Challenge of Women's Studies." In *Georgetown at Two Hundred: Faculty Reflections on the University's Future,* edited by W. C. McFadden. Washington, D.C.: Georgetown University Press, 1990.

Fitzgerald, Robert, SJ. *The Soul of Sponsorship: The Friendship of Fr. Ed Dowling, S.J., and Bill Wilson in Letters.* Center City, Minn.: Hazelden-Pittman Archives Press, 1995.

Ford, Corrine. *We Follow Jesus.* Confraternity of Christian Doctrine Edition. Book 3. New York: Benziger Bros., 1967.

Franzen, Jonathan. *The Corrections.* New York: Farrar, Straus and Giroux, 2001.

General Catechetical Directory. Washington, D.C.: United States Catholic Conference, 1971.

Gibson, Mel. *The Passion of the Christ.* An Icon Production, 2004.

Gilson, Etienne. *Painting and Reality.* New York: Pantheon Books, 1957.

Golding, William. *The Lord of the Flies.* New York: Berkley, 2003.

Greeley, Andrew. *The Catholic Imagination.* Berkeley: University of California Press, 2000.

Hart, David B. "Christ and Nothing," *First Things* 136 (October 2003): 47–57.

Hitchcock, James.*The Decline and Fall of Radical Catholicism.* New York: Herder & Herder, 1971.

————. "Guilt and the Moral Revolution." In *Years of Crisis: Collected Essays 1970–1983.* San Francisco: Ignatius Press; Harrison, N.Y.: Roman Catholic Books, 1985.

————. *The Pope and the Jesuits: John Paul II and the New Order in the Society of Jesus.* With an introduction by Joseph Sobran. New York: National Center of Catholic Laymen, 1984.

————. "The Root of American Violence." In *Years of Crisis: Collected Essays 1970–1983.* San Francisco: Ignatius Press, Harrison, N.Y.: Roman Catholic Books, 1985.

Ignatius Loyola. *The Spiritual Exercises of St. Ignatius.* With an introduction by Robert W. Gleason. Translated by Anthony Mottola. Garden City, N.Y.: Image Books, 1964.

John Paul II. Apostolic Exhortation *Catechesi Tradendae* (On Catechesis in Our Time). October 16, 1979. In *The Post-Synodal Apostolic Exhortations of John Paul II.* Edited and with an introduction by J. Michael Miller. Huntington, Ind.: Our Sunday Visitor, 1998.

————. *Crossing the Threshold of Hope.* Edited by Vittorio Messori. Translated by Jenny McPhee and Martha McPhee. New York: Knopf, 1994.

————. Encyclical Letter *Veritatis Splendor* (*The Splendor of Truth*). August 6, 1993. Boston: Pauline Books and Media, 1993.

————. *The Theology of the Body: Human Love in the Divine Plan.* With a foreword by John S. Grabowski. Boston: Pauline Books and Media, 1997.

Johnson, Paul. *Intellectuals.* New York: Harper Perennial, 1990.

Kurtz, Ernest. *Not-God: A History of Alcoholics Anonymous.* Center City, Minn.: Hazelden Educational Services, 1979.

Larson, Eric. *The Devil in the White City: Murder, Magic, and Madness at the Fair that Changed America.* New York: Crown, 2003.

Lewis, C. S. *The Chronicles of Narnia.* New York: HarperCollins, 2000.

————. *The Four Loves.* New York: Harcourt Brace Jovanovich, 1991.

————. *The Screwtape Letters.* New York: Macmillan, 1944.

Martin, Malachi. *The Jesuits: The Society of Jesus and the Betrayal of the Roman Catholic Church.* New York: Linden Press, Simon & Schuster, 1987.

McNeil, John J. *The Church and the Homosexual.* Kansas City, Kans.: Sheed Andrews & McMeel, 1976.

Menand, Louis. "Life in the Stone Age." *New Republic* 7 (January 14, 1991): 38–44.

Merton, Thomas. "Christian Humanism." *Spiritual Life,* 1967.

———. *No Man Is an Island.* New York: Harcourt Brace, 1955.

———. *The Seven Storey Mountain.* 50th anniversary ed. New York: Harcourt Brace, 1998.

Moran, Brother Gabriel. "Catechetics, R.I.P." *Commonweal* 1970.

Mueller, Francis John. *The Faith in Action.* Milwaukee: Bruce, 1952.

National Conference of Catholic Bishops. *Basic Teachings for Catholic Religious Education.* Washington, D.C.: United States Catholic Conference, 1973.

Neuhaus, Richard John. *Death on a Friday Afternoon: Meditations on the Last Words of Jesus from the Cross.* New York: Basic Books, 2000.

Nietzsche, Friedrich. *The Birth of Tragedy.* Translated by Clifton P. Fadiman. New York: Dover Publications, 1995.

———. *The Genealogy of Morals.* Translated by Horace B. Samuel. New York: Boni & Liveright, 1918.

Novak, Michael. *A New Generation: American and Catholic.* New York: Herder & Herder, 1964.

Paul VI. Encyclical Letter *Humanae Vitae* (*On the Regulation of Births*). July 25, 1968. Washington, D.C.: United States Catholic Conference, 1968.

Peck, M. Scott. *The Road Less Traveled.* Kansas City, Mo.: Andrews McMeel, 2001.

Pieper, Josef. *The Four Cardinal Virtues: Prudence, Justice, Fortitude, Temperance.* Translated by Richard and Clara Winston and others. New York: Harcourt, Brace & World, 1965.

———. *In Tune with the World: A Theory of Festivity.* Translated by Richard and Clara Winston. South Bend, Ind.: St. Augustine's Press, 1999.

———. "The Obscurity of Hope and Despair." In *Josef Pieper: An Anthology.* San Francisco: Ignatius Press, 1989.

———. *On Hope.* Translated by Mary Frances McCarthy. San Francisco: Ignatius Press, 1986.

———. *On Love.* In *Faith, Hope, Love.* San Francisco: Ignatius Press, 1997.

Pius XII. Encyclical Letter *Humani Generis* (Concerning Some False Opinions Threatening to Undermine the Foundations of Catholic Doctrine). August 12, 1950. *The Encyclical "Humani Generis": With a Commentary by A. C. Cotter.* Weston, Mass.: Weston College Press, 1951.

———. Encyclical Letter *Mediator Dei* (On the Sacred Liturgy). November 20, 1947. *On the Sacred Liturgy: Encyclical Letter ("Mediator Dei") of Pope Pius XII.* With an introduction and notes by Gerald Ellard. New York: America Press, 1948.

Powers, Ann. *Weird Like Us: My Bohemian America.* New York: Simon & Schuster, 2000.

Ratzinger, Joseph Cardinal, and Christoph Schönborn. *A Turning Point for Europe? The Church in the Modern World: Assessment and Forecast.* San Francisco: Ignatius Press, 1994.

Reese, Thomas J., SJ, ed. *The Universal Catechism Reader: Reflections and Responses.* San Francisco: HarperCollins, 1990.

Ryan, Mary Perkins. *Are Parochial Schools the Answer? Catholic Education in the Light of the Council.* New York: Holt, Rinehart & Winston, 1964.

Salinger, J. D. *The Catcher in the Rye.* Boston: Little, Brown, 1951.

Sertillanges, A. G. *The Intellectual Life: Its Spirits, Conditions, Methods.* Translated by Mary Ryan. Westminster, Md.: Newman Press, 1959.

Sheed, Frank. *The Church and I.* Garden City, N.Y.: Doubleday, 1974.

————. *Theology and Sanity.* New York: Sheed & Ward, 1946.

Sheen, Fulton J. *Life of Christ.* New York: McGraw-Hill, 1958.

Sloyan, Gerard S. *How Do I Know I'm Doing Right? Toward the Formation of a Christian Conscience.* Christian Experience Series. New York: Pflaum, 1976.

Sullivan, Thomas F. *A Discussion Guide to Sharing the Light of Faith.* Washington, D.C.: National Conference of Diocesan Directors of Religious Education, 1979.

————, and John F. Meyers. *Focus on American Catechetics: A Commentary on the"General Catechetical Directory."* Washington, D.C.: NCEA National Conference of Directors of Religious Education, 1972.

Tolkien, J. R. R. *The Lord of the Rings.* London: Allen & Unwin, 1954–55.

United States Catholic Conference. *Sharing the Light of Faith: National Catechetical Directory for Catholics of the United States.* Washington, D.C.: United States Catholic Conference, 1979.

————, Division of Religious Education-CCD. *A Study Aid for Basic Teachings for Catholic Religious Education.* Edited by Berard I. Marthaler and V. A. Brooks. Washington, D.C.: United States Catholic Conference, 1974.

Von Hildebrand, Alice. *The Soul of a Lion: Dietrich Von Hildebrand: A Biography.* San Francisco: Ignatius Press, 2000.

Von Hildebrand, Dietrich. "Beauty in the Light of the Redemption." Reprinted in *Logos: A Journal of Catholic Thought and Culture* 4, no. 2 (Spring 2001): 78–92.

————. *The Charitable Anathema.* Fort Collins, Colo.: Roman Catholic Books, 1993.

————. *Transformation in Christ: On the Christian Attitude.* San Francisco: Ignatius Press, 2001.

————. *Trojan Horse in the City of God.* Chicago: Franciscan Herald Press, 1967.

Warren, Michael, ed. *Sourcebook for Modern Catechetics.* Winona, Minn.: St. Mary's Press, Christian Brothers Publications, 1983.

Waugh, Evelyn. *Brideshead Revisited.* London: Chapman & Hall, 1945.

Weigel, George. *Letters to a Young Catholic.* New York: Basic Books, 2004.

————. *Witness to Hope: The Biography of Pope John Paul II.* New York: Cliff Street Books, 1999.

Wilhelm, Anthony. *Christ Among Us.* San Francisco: Harper & Row, 1985.

Williams, Charles. *All Hallows Eve.* With an introduction by T. S. Eliot. New York: Pellegrini & Cudahy, 1948.

W[ilson], Bill. *Twelve Steps and Twelve Traditions.* New York: Alcoholics Anonymous Publishing, 1953.

Wrenn, Msgr. Michael J. *Catechisms and Controversies: Religious Education in the Postconciliar Years.* San Francisco: Ignatius Press, 1991.

————, and Kenneth D. Whitehead. "The Translation of the Catechism." *Crisis,* November 1993.

Wright, John J. *Resonare Christum: A Selection from the Sermons, Addresses, Interviews, and Prayers of Cardinal John J. Wright.* Prepared and edited by R. Stephen Almagno. 3 vols. San Francisco: Ignatius Press, 1985–95.

Index of
Authors and Titles

179

Of Related Interest

Deal Hudson
AN AMERICAN CONVERSION
One Man's Discovery of Beauty and Truth in Times of Crisis

Crisis magazine publisher, syndicated radio host, and frequent guest on national media, Hudson offers his memoir of the beauty and truth of the Catholic faith as seen through the eyes of one of today's most prominent converts.

0-8245-2126-9, $22.95 hardcover

Father Richard John Neuhaus
APPOINTMENT IN ROME
The Church in America Awakening

"I have never before read an account quite like this of any Synod: candid, pungent, yet confidently hopeful. I learned much from *Appointment in Rome* about the Synod of America, even though I had faithfully attended every session."
— John Cardinal O'Connor, Archbishop of New York

0-8245-1555-2, $24.95 hardcover

Please support your local bookstore,
or call 1-800-707-0670 for Customer Service.

For a free catalog, write us at

THE CROSSROAD PUBLISHING COMPANY
16 Penn Plaza, 481 Eighth Avenue
New York, NY 10001

All prices subject to change.

crossroad

The Crossroad Publishing Company is delighted to welcome Mark Gauvreau Judge to our house.

Mark is best known for his incisive writing on American pop culture and Catholicism. His widest audience has been younger readers who have followed his trademark style in his writings for the *Wall Street Journal, New York Press, Crisis*, and other media. Prior to *God and Man at Georgetown Prep*, his best-known work had been his study of Washington D.C.'s professional baseball team, *Damn Senators*.

Mark lives in Washington, D.C. He can be reached for speaking engagements via Crossroad at rgreer@crossroadpublishing.com.